The Tug Hill Program

Note: At the time the book was completed, March 1980,
the Temporary State Commission on Tug Hill had proposed its termination. It had initiated a process at the
local level to determine what parts of the program
were worth continuing and, if any, by what means.
State and local review has resulted in a legislated extension of the Commission for five years beginning
August 1, 1981.

A New York State Study

Inman Gulf. *Photograph courtesy of Peter J. Jerome.*

1981

The Tug Hill Program

A Regional Planning Option for Rural Areas

CYNTHIA D. DYBALLA
LYLE S. RAYMOND, Jr.
ALAN J. HAHN

Syracuse University Press   1981

Copyright © 1981 by SYRACUSE UNIVERSITY PRESS
Syracuse, New York 13210

The work upon which this publication is based was supported in part by the Temporary State Commission on Tug Hill, Watertown, New York.

Library of Congress Cataloging in Publication Data
Dyballa, Cynthia D.

The Tug Hill program.

(A New York State study)
Includes bibliographical references and index.
1. Regional planning—New York (State)—Tug Hill region—Case studies. 2. Rural development—New York (State)—Tug Hill region—Case studies. I. Raymond, Lyle S. II. Hahn, Alan J. (Alan Joseph), 1940–
III. Title. IV. Series: New York State study.
HT393.N72T833   361.6′09747′5   81-8999
ISBN 0-8156-2241-4   AACR2

Contents

MAPS

FIGURE

TABLES

CYNTHIA D. DYBALLA received the M.P.S. in natural resources policy/planning from Cornell University and has done comparative study of the Adirondack Park Agency, Tug Hill Commission, and Catskill Commission. She is Regional Community Resource Development Specialist, Cooperative Extension Service, Norfolk County, Massachusetts.

ALAN J. HAHN is Associate Professor, College of Human Ecology, Cornell University. His interests lie in community decision-making and state-local and federal-local relations. He has been involved in studies of the Adirondack Park Agency and Tug Hill and Catskill commissions, and has worked on the Cooperative Extension MIDNY Project.

LYLE S. RAYMOND, Jr., was raised in the Tug Hill area and worked on the Cooperative Extension MIDNY Project and the Hudson River Valley Commission. He is currently working in the water resources field at the Center for Environmental Research, Cornell University.

Acknowledgments

THIS STUDY was partially funded by the Temporary State Commission on Tug Hill as part of its phase-out program. The study would not have been possible, however, without the active cooperation of the many fine folks in the Tug Hill towns who provided information and consented to interviews. A special thanks goes to Joe "Squash" for providing Cynthia Dyballa with a tour of Tug Hill's interior reaches, contributing an added dimension to the field work phase of the project.

The cooperation of the commissioners of the Tug Hill Commission and the Commission staff, who shared their information and consented to lengthy interviews, also contributed significantly to the study results. The impetus for this study owes a great deal to the Commission's executive director, Benjamin Coe.

Research was coordinated through the Cornell University Center for Environmental Research, which also provided administrative and secretarial support. We also wish to acknowledge, with appreciation, the helpful suggestions, criticisms, and insights contributed by interested members of the Cornell University faculty.

Finally, on behalf of Cynthia Dyballa, a word of thanks to Maryanne Frangulis and Leonard Seligman for their support and encouragement.

Preface

THE TEMPORARY STATE COMMISSION ON TUG HILL was created in 1972 by the New York State Legislature. It was charged with recommending policies for natural resource protection and development of a thirty-nine-town rural area of 1,285,000 acres in portions of four counties (see Map 1). This study area is centered on the Tug Hill upland, which rises to more than 1,900 feet elevation about 25 miles east of Lake Ontario. Tug Hill is the local folk-name for the highest portions of this upland, which are heavily forested and sparsely populated. The entire area's 1970 population was 81,521.

The Tug Hill Commission's approach to rural planning and development for the past eight years represents a synthesis of various methods. Some of its activities depart from conventional approaches to rural resource issues. As such, they represent an alternative possibly unusual method for coping with rural resource management.

This study concentrates on what the Tug Hill Commission did, whether it worked, and why. The purposes of this report are:

1. to describe the Tug Hill program as a whole, emphasizing what has been tried, the philosophy behind it, and how it differs from other strategies for rural planning and development;

2. to describe the significant events and the setting contributing to development of the Tug Hill program; and

3. to examine the successes and failures of this approach in a practical manner for possible application to rural planning and development programs in other areas.

No final solutions to the issues of rural planning and development are offered here; the Commission program is but one alterna-

Map I
The Tug Hill Study Area in
New York State

tive, suitable in some situations and not others. The study concludes, however, with a list of lessons learned from this program.

Several considerations are important in assessing the Commission's successes and failures. Having no regulatory power, the Commission has had to rely on its ability to influence the decisions of local governments. Thus one major concern is whether the Commission has influenced the local decision-making process and if so, how this was done. In addition, since it depends on state funding, the Commission has also had to convince state-level policy makers that its programs serve state interests in the area. Thus state-level responses to the Commission's program are also explored. Finally, a third consideration is attitudes of other county and state agencies that must work with the Commission.

Although some attention is given to the cost of the Commission's program, effectiveness of land use regulations established, and other results of the Commission's activities in the Tug Hill area, this study is descriptive and does not include a formal evaluation of the Commission's policies. Likewise, a thorough comparison of the Commission's approach to those of other similar agencies is beyond the scope of this study. We have, however, provided some thoughts on this subject for those with interests in this aspect of the Commission's work.

This report is designed to be read by a variety of county- and state-level officials, legislators, staff, planners, academics, and other persons who are involved in deciding policy and programs for rural areas. For state-level policy makers, it is a reminder that top-down planning is only one approach, and there are alternatives. For local decision-makers, it provides suggestions on how to cope with outside pressures, including the intervention of higher-level government. The success of the Commission's overall approach and many of the techniques involved should also be useful to administrators of a variety of higher level organizations working in rural areas.

This report was prepared by staff at Cornell University. It was funded through a contract with the Temporary State Commission on Tug Hill for an independent review of its programs, as part of its phase-out activities. Cynthia D. Dyballa, Research Support Specialist with Cornell's Center for Environmental Research, conducted the field research and prepared the draft manuscript. Project direction and editing were performed by Project Managers Lyle S. Raymond, Jr., Water Resources Information Specialist at the Cornell Center for Environmental Research, and Alan J. Hahn, Associate Professor of Political Science, Department of Human Service Studies, College of Human Ecology.

Sixty field interviews were conducted with local officials, planning board members, and residents as well as county, regional, and state-level employees and officials. Much of the information in this report is drawn from these interviews and is not directly attributed to individuals, to protect their confidentiality.

One final note: the Tug Hill Commission is presently authorized until March 31, 1981. Research for this report was completed in March 1980. Since the Commission has not yet completed its work, this is a review of a program still in progress. Many issues regarding the program's long-term success cannot be resolved for some time to come. This report captures the Commission's work at one moment in time.

Cynthia D. Dyballa
Lyle S. Raymond, Jr.
Alan J. Hahn

The Tug Hill Program

1 In Quest of Workable Rural Planning and Development Options

THE SPECIAL NATURE OF RURAL AREAS

ALTHOUGH THE MAJORITY OF PEOPLE in the United States reside in urban and suburban areas, rural areas dominate the national landscape. Often perceived by metropolitan residents as the land "left behind" when other land uses are accounted for, rural areas instead provide the natural resource base both for metropolitan populations and for the entire nation. As phrased by one leading rural planner, "Rural society is not just a low density area in the process of becoming urban."[1]

Not surprisingly, rural areas, and the people who live in them, differ from more populous metropolitan areas in many respects. Both a rural region's economic base and its land use patterns may vary markedly from those of metropolitan regions. The greater land area supports a more dispersed population, marked by occasional small concentrations of people living and working in rural service centers. In the northeastern United States mixed land use patterns are common, though forests and active agricultural lands often dominate the visual landscape.

Rural people are more likely to earn their living directly or indirectly from the area's natural resources, although in many rural areas a substantial number of residents are either retired or commuters to nearby urban centers. The people of a rural area may be a more homogeneous group than their metropolitan counterparts. Long-run change in these areas tends to occur more slowly. The pace of life often appears less rushed, as activities are spread across the landscape.

Attitudes toward the land owned and used in rural areas often reflect different values from those prevalent in urban areas. Land is not only a commodity with development potential and value but useful in its existing state as a natural resource. Local physical attractions can figure highly in why rural residents stay in an area or are attracted to it as migrants from urban areas.

Local politics in a rural area is often highly personal and informal, deals with more concrete issues, and attracts participation of fewer organized groups but more direct involvement of individuals. Local governments, in almost all states, are the primary units of government responsible for promoting the common interest in rural land and its uses. Yet rural local governments are beset with a variety of problems and limitations, many not of their own making, that can often restrict their ability to influence effectively the use of land.

Many rural officials are part-time, busy with other jobs, and able to devote only limited time to municipal affairs. With low population, large land area, and often low tax income, many rural towns have little money to work with. Part-time local officials often have little technical, administrative, or financial training for their jobs. This applies to some who have held office for many years. The U.S. Advisory Commission on Intergovernmental Relations identified this situation more than ten years ago: "Rural governmental institutions are frequently unable to provide the type of public services needed. They were originally designed with less acute problems in an age of greater self-sufficiency. . . . Furthermore, the small local governments are frequently ill-equipped to undertake the planning and development activities necessary to overcome their handicaps."[2]

Rural local governments have not generally considered zoning, other forms of land use control, or planning to be effective ways of managing land. Planning boards, where they exist, are frequently created to solve specific problems, not to shape long-term land use policies. And often residents of rural towns strongly resist government involvement at any level in land use issues. One Tug Hill local planning board member described the difficulty of the board's task: "We've got one night, and they're mad when they come, to teach them why we need zoning."

At the same time, rural local government officials must cope with increasingly complex issues. Development pressures on much agricultural and other types of rural land, often from outside the

Moore's General Store, Lorraine. *Photograph courtesy of W. H. Kennedy, Jr.*

immediate area, have increased. So has deterioration in land and water quality in some rural areas. People from nearby cities and from large metropolitan areas some distance away have also increased recreational pressures on many rural lands. State and federal regulations and requirements for local governments, particularly for environmental protection, have increased. Many metropolitan residents now support programs for preserving some rural lands, and often new rural residents or landowners want to halt additional development in their area.

Thus rural towns may feel many outside pressures regarding recreation, preservation, development, and government management. It is not hard to see how local governments may feel powerless against these overwhelming outside forces.[3]

ISSUES AND OPTIONS IN RURAL RESOURCE MANAGEMENT

While a strong desire exists in many rural towns to retain local control of land use decisions, these decisions increasingly have broader ramifications. Richard Babcock, speaking generally of local government, put it this way: "The flaw is that the criteria for decision-making are exclusively local, even when the interests are far more comprehensive."[4]

Many states, and to an extent the federal government, are expressing interest in influencing rural land use to protect the statewide public interest, citing the "parochial" nature of local governments. According to the U.S. Advisory Commission on Intergovernmental Relations, "In terms of the governance systems, nonmetropolitan areas tend to equal or surpass the jurisdictional fragmentation of urban America."[5] Rationales given for this state involvement include: the broad scope of environmental issues, the perceived inadequacies of small rural local governments, the greater resources of state professional staff, the perceived advantages of an areawide perspective, and the importance of protecting the rural landscape for metropolitan Americans.[6]

Time and again, creation of a regional organization has been suggested as the best way for a higher level of government to treat the multitude of rural issues and to influence local decisions, especially in the area of land use planning and development. These regional bodies are often developed in response to interests expressed by those who cannot satisfy their needs through the existing fragmented rural local government structure.[7]

Yet many professionals have discovered that conventional planning, zoning, and economic development methods are not effective in rural areas, particularly as practiced on a regional basis by outsiders from the state or federal government. A number of authors have written of the inadequacies of these methods in prompting change in rural communities. Yet few have proposed an alternative. This question of how to approach the problem is a central one.

Some groups have defined rural issues in economic terms. This has resulted in strategies both for regional economic development and for building up the local economy through a variety of local development techniques. Others have focused on provision of social services, such as improved health care. Other emphases have been on traditional land use planning and, more recently, on planning and regulation to protect an area's natural resources. And still others see the underlying issue of rural areas as one of self-determination. This approach emphasizes education, community organizing, leadership development, or clarification of local values, with minimal emphasis on satisfying outside interests.

There also exist several options for carrying out these strategies. But there is one main choice: a bottom-up or top-down approach. This choice has been described as follows from a state-level perspective: "States have two major options for dealing with the inability of local governments in rural areas to perform necessary public functions and provide needed public services. They can bolster rural local governments, or they can substantially supplement them and/or supplant them."[8] Self-help and local assistance options, primarily facilitative, seek to bolster rural local governments. More authoritative methods involve a high degree of rule setting, regulation, and assumption of decision-making power by the regulatory agency. At one extreme, a regulatory approach can provoke such local hostility that it cannot function effectively. At the other extreme, strictly local efforts may not actually improve local government capabilities.

Another local author recently gave this description of Tug Hill: "To begin with, Tug Hill is not actually a hill at all, at least not a hill that one may climb, and resting on the crest, say to oneself, 'I have reached the top.'* . . . Instead, Tug Hill Country embraces not only the plateau itself, but all the vast regions that are watered by and drained from the tumultous streams that come down from its flinty slopes and through its rocky gorges."[3]

Yet a 1974 report confirmed what many area residents have known for years: that Tug Hill, for many, is always "somewhere over there."[4] Historically, the central Tug Hill area carried a negative image, especially in Black River farm towns. But core area residents often identify strongly with Tug Hill and its resources.

Tug Hill is geologically the remains of an ancient plateau, as is the Appalachian upland in southern New York, with which it is often associated in landform descriptions. This has contributed to popular description of Tug Hill as a plateau, especially in the last fifty years.

*This is more clearly true on the west side, where the author resided, than on the east, where a prominent escarpment overlooks the Black River Valley.

From here to p. 10 belong is Chap. 2, right after text

Looking east from the Tug Hill upland, with the fertile Black River Valley in background and Whetstone Gulf State Park in foreground. (Gorges are often called gulfs in northern New York.) *Photograph courtesy of David M. Doody.*

Hiking down Lorraine Gulf. Ten thousand years ago, when the glacier from the last ice age receded, the Tug Hill gorges were carved, exposing a layered natural history. *Photograph courtesy of John L. Osinski.*

The Tug Hill upland begins 10 to 15 miles from Lake Ontario (245 feet elevation) and rises gently eastward to a maximum elevation of approximately 2,100 feet, 35 miles from the lake. Tug Hill is capped with sandstone which is more resistant to erosion than the shale and limestone which underlies the major portion of the hill at a lower depth. The escarpment formed at this eastern edge drops sharply as a series of terraces 1,100 to 1,300 feet from the crest to the Black River, 6 to 7 miles away.[5] According to local folklore, this escarpment accounts for the area's name: "tugging" up the steep hill from the Black River, a major transportation corridor during the settlement period (see Map 2).

The Tug Hill environment is harsh and wet. Three of the state's major rivers—the Mohawk, Black, and Oswego—are fed by runoff

MAP 2

Tug Hill Study Area Topography

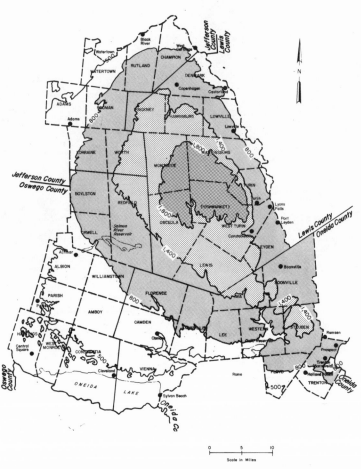

Scale in Miles
0   5   10

Contour Elevations in Feet As Indicated

Highest Point is Gomer Hill, Town of Turin, 2115 Feet

Source: Temporary State Commission on Tug Hill, _Preparing for the Future_ (Watertown, N.Y. 1975)

MAP 3
Population of Tug Hill Study Area Towns, 1970

Source: Temporary State Commission on Tug Hill, _Interim Report_ (Watertown, N.Y., 1974)

from the Tug Hill upland. Several smaller watersheds draining into Lake Ontario also originate here; the largest of these are the Salmon River, Sandy Creek, and South Sandy Creek. The core area receives an annual average of 200 to 300 inches of snow, up to an extreme of 466.9 inches in 1967–77 (a new state snowfall record). This, reportedly the highest annual snowfall east of the Rocky Mountains, is primarily the result of severe lake-effect storms.[6] The growing season is short. Soils are thin, stony, poorly drained, and acidic at the upper elevations.[7]

Intermediate courses are also possible. Here, again, there are many options, including: studying the issues at hand and advising on them in the role of expert; defining alternatives for local action; forming some partnership between local and outside decisionmakers; or organizing local people for action.

The degree of federal, state, county, and local involvement in structures for managing rural affairs ranges from strictly local, encouraging informal cooperation on particular issues, to a regional or even statewide scale. The range of structures includes state line agencies, temporary state commissions, special regional regulatory agencies, regional planning or economic development boards, voluntary councils of government comprised primarily of local officials, local government consolidation or contracts, private nonprofit organizations, and many others.

Finally, the type and timing of results expected from these efforts vary greatly. Some efforts, such as regional regulation, anticipate immediate overall changes; others focus on a specific project, such as highway construction. And some strive for gradual, incremental change from existing conditions, with flexible goals.

REGIONAL ORGANIZATIONS IN RURAL AREAS

The number of regional agencies designed to tackle rural issues has grown markedly since the early 1960s.[9] Some have been created in response to increased federal incentives or requirements through areawide mandates and grant programs. These regional organizations often act as links to local governments for administering specific federal programs. A substantial number perform the federally mandated A-95 function of areawide project review.

Central Tug Hill averages more than 200 inches of snow per winter. During the winter of 1976–77, the year of "the blizzard," thirty-eight feet of snow fell. *Photograph courtesy of W. H. Kennedy, Jr.*

Many states view regionalization as a partial solution to balancing state and local concerns for rural resource use. Nearly all fifty states, including New York, have established systems of substate districts for regional planning and development, which include rural areas. In a few states, these district agencies concentrate many rural programs under one roof. But rural areas are often served by several competing areawide agencies, each with its own program, mission, and funding sources.

And many regional organizations formed by local elected officials are not independent of higher-level intervention. Most states add a financial "buy-in" contribution to federal program dollars, which together can force specific program requirements to be met.

Most regional organizations have concentrated on problems of rural areas from one of three major perspectives: economic development, land use planning, or environmental protection. We briefly outline these three perspectives and note further references for the interested reader.

ECONOMIC DEVELOPMENT

Beginning with U.S. Department of Agriculture economic planning efforts in the 1940s, strengthening the economies of rural areas has been a concern primarily of federal and state governments.[10] This aid has taken several forms. Much of it concentrates on construction of physical facilities and public works, which can channel money into a rural economy. Another focus has been on bolstering local agriculture and providing economic back up for farmers.

Implicit in many of these economic development strategies is the idea that rural areas are backward, depressed, not fully integrated into the mainstream of American life, and should be developed to utilize their full potential. One planner noted of rural economic development efforts, "Backward meant poor, and poor almost aways meant rural."[11] Another assumption is the benefit of encouraging concentrated development in growth centers within particular rural areas.

An early example of regional authority to aid a depressed rural area is the Tennessee Valley Authority (TVA), created in the 1930s as the first comprehensive river basin development project. TVA was to integrate natural resource development to advance a rural area's economy and provide needed power for urban residents.[12] Another significant federal effort to bolster a depressed rural economy is that of the Appalachian Regional Commission (ARC), created in 1965 at the request of a group of governors to provide links to federal financial assistance, allocate federal aid, and coordinate regional economic development planning. Besides the ARC, six other multistate regional commissions operate, though at a much lower funding level.[13]

Many state programs for rural economic development have followed the federal lead of concentrating aid to particular depressed areas. A focus of many state planners, until recently, has been efforts to attract industrial or commercial development to rural areas. Two recent trends have emerged. One focuses on area self-sufficiency. Small-scale, locally selected and controlled, natural resource based development is urged as an alternative to developing rural areas as subsets of metropolitan regions. Another recent emphasis is on energy resource development, particularly in rural western states.

LAND USE PLANNING

Land use planning is another common approach to improving rural local governments' capabilities. But most federal and state planning programs have focused on metropolitan regions. Rural planning, as a separate field, barely exists. Only recently did the major national professional planning organization form a branch of rural and community planning. William R. Lassey recently wrote, "Planning for rural regions is primitive indeed as a body of integrated concepts.[14] Most efforts have followed conventional urban or regional planning methods, adapted from theories assuming the need for an urban center of development. One agricultural economist terms this "urbocentric planning."[15]

Increasingly, however, rural planning methods are tied to theories of environmental planning based on natural land capabilities, such as those espoused by Ian McHarg.[16] For example, efforts at the University of Vermont encourage communities to plan from their natural resource base. This particular approach also emphasizes developing local public goals.[17]

Land use planning in most of the fifty states is a local power, granted by state enabling legislation. But federal influence has been exerted through several major federal programs, encouraging both local and areawide planning in metropolitan and rural areas. Most significant is "701" funding through the 1954 Comprehensive Planning Assistance Program, with its accompanying technical guidelines and requirements for areawide and local planning.[18]

At least nine substantially rural states, including Idaho, Montana, Oregon, and Wyoming, have mandated statewide local land use planning, sometimes with provisions for state planning where local governments do not implement regulations.[19] Maine's state-level Land Use Regulation Commission determines planning, zoning, and subdivision controls for all of Maine's rural unorganized areas. Going a step further, Hawaii has implemented a statewide zoning system.[20] Other states' strategies include passing along federal planning funds, providing technical assistance through state community development agencies, or fostering rural local planning through regional planning and development boards. While some states encourage local land use planning to limit growth in rural areas, others foster it to attract growth.

A recent trend in both local and areawide land use planning for rural areas is increased federal and state emphasis on citizen involvement. At least two states, Massachusetts and Washington, have attempted to form statewide growth policies through a wide ranging citizen education and involvement program, reaching even rural citizens who might normally lack input into such plans.[21]

ENVIRONMENTAL PROTECTION

Rural environmental concerns have taken several forms: promotion of land use planning and management, regional organization, regulation for air and water quality, and legislation aimed at specific environmental areas or problems. Three common methods for land use management are: identification and regulation of critical natural and rural areas; comprehensive regional land use zoning, such as Hawaii's state management system; and regional or state control of development projects.

Identification and regulation of critical natural areas, such as wetlands or shoreline, have been widely advanced through the American Law Institute's Model Land Use Development Code. For example, Florida employs a statewide identification of critical areas.[22]

More as a result of outside interest in preserving farmlands for aesthetics rather than food production, a number of states have embarked on some form of agricultural preservation program for many rural areas. These include tax policies, formation of agricultural districts, and purchase of development rights.

Other states have adopted a combination of regional planning, regulation, and mandated local planning systems for critical natural areas. New York's Adirondack Park Agency (APA) and the bistate Lake Tahoe Regional Planning Agency are examples.[23] The APA prepared both private and public land use plans for a six-million-acre region, with private land use controlled by a regional permit system. Coastal zone management programs, many begun in response to the federal 1972 Coastal Zone Management Act, now affect rural areas in thirty states.[24]

A few primarily rural states, such as Vermont and Maine, have adopted statewide systems of regional planning commissions and/or review of development projects, according to state land use standards for development.[25] While encouraging and even requiring local land use planning, statewide permit systems are often motivated by a desire at the state level for environmental protection and growth control, rather than support for local-level decision-making.

A number of states have embarked on some form of critical area program for preserving agricultural lands. This has happened more as a result of outside interest in aesthetics rather than in food production. The programs may include tax policy changes, formation of agricultural districts, and purchase of development rights.

LIMITS TO CONVENTIONAL APPROACHES

All three of these strategies—economic development, land use planning, and environmental protection—have been criticized as not successful in rural areas, and not effective in building the capabilities of rural governments.

Both local economic development efforts and areawide economic development planning, as traditionally practiced, have been criticized as inappropriate for small rural communities. Urban strategies designed for large communities with strong competing interest groups do not take into account the smaller scale, different economic base, greater social cohesion, and traditional functions of rural communities. One study of small rural towns noted, "The concepts used to both study and assist small towns are often urban in nature and do not fit well small town realities."[26]

Conventional local and regional planning methods for rural areas have come under serious attack, even from members of the planning profession. The appropriateness of urban techniques, originally designed for use in metropolitan communities, is questioned.

The complex language and segregated land uses of zoning and the predominant implementation technique of many plans do not fit the needs of many rural communities. And attitudes of planners and other professionals, perhaps more appropriate in sophisticated urban areas, appear elitist, overly technical, and patronizing to many rural local officials. In particular, a lack of communication has often been cited between planners and rural organizations.

Methods of regional planning and regulation for environmental protection in rural areas have also proved to be of limited effectiveness. A number of examples of well-functioning regional land use programs exist, but other programs have failed for political reasons, primarily opposition of rural residents to regional land use controls that were perceived as representing outside interests at the expense of local. Experience has shown that development of regional regulations must proceed with the consent of those to be regulated, as well as outside interested parties. Without this consent, regulations become eroded in the long term. Yet there has been little attention to this fact in development of most land use regulation systems.

Land use regulation is viewed by many local officials as a negative strategy, preventing actions rather than encouraging them. Many also complain that, without some form of assistance to administer these regulations at the local level, this increased workload creates inefficiency and unmanageable local government, particularly in rural areas.

Methods of citizen involvement in all three approaches have also come under attack. Even organizations with extensive citizen participation programs on paper have been criticized for contacting the public and local officials only after their work is essentially complete.

Finally, the fact that many regional organizations are established or induced by higher levels of government raises additional difficulties. Statewide constituencies may have goals for the regions in question that conflict with local preferences. How does the agency balance state, local, and outside interests? Who decides? Who determines the size of the region and its boundaries? Should the regional agency have regulatory powers or only advisory ones? How much involvement and influence should local governments and region citizens have? To whom should the agency be accountable? There are no simple answers to these questions.

THE TUG HILL APPROACH: An Alternative?

The Temporary State Commission on Tug Hill, one of several regional bodies created by the New York State Legislature to identify ways to guide land use and development and improve natural resource management in rural areas of the state, has developed an approach that contrasts with more accepted regional planning methods which emphasize adoption of regional standards or regulations.[27] By working with region residents and governments and responding to their needs, the Commission has evolved a cooperative, intermunicipal method for planning and development.

Undeveloped relative to nearby urban areas, Tug Hill has recently experienced rising development and recreational pressures. Local land use controls, where they existed at all, were not adequate to cope with large-scale outside development. Part-time local officials noted in interviews that they lacked technical training, money, and the time needed to resolve, and sometimes to recognize, the broad scope of issues affecting them, despite a strong interest in preservation of the area.[28] The Tug Hill Commission's executive director once described Tug Hill towns as "resource rich but tax poor." Further, some people look on Tug Hill as a natural area of special significance within the state.[29]

The Tug Hill Commission has often been viewed as a regional planning agency. But it has expanded beyond its original assignment as a study commission, as well as beyond the conventional approach to regional land use planning for rural areas, to undertake a variety of services to local governments in an effort to support their total capability. Its present multiple-approach program incorporates elements of several disciplines: land use planning, rural community development, economic development, local government administration, and education.

The Commission's program emphasizes helping rural local governments direct their own affairs more capably. But the Commission is more than a service agency to local governments. It also influences them to take actions they might not have taken without higher-level assistance, particularly in land use planning and control. Its mandate and the fact of its creation and continuation by the state require that it somehow satisfy state as well as local interests.

Thus the Tug Hill Commission's program can be viewed as an

effort to integrate state and local concerns to meet some of the needs of a rural area. It is the process the Commission has employed, particularly its interaction with local governments, that presents a possible alternative to other approaches. While most elements of this approach are not unusual, their synthesis in the Commission's programs for this area is. Interest in the Commission's activities is sparked by the fact that only a few workable and locally acceptable methods for rural planning presently exist, and that the Commission appears to have achieved some success in its decentralized approach.

2 The Tug Hill Commission: Its Context

THIS BOOK FOCUSES on the Tug Hill Commission's program and its possible application to other rural areas. Consideration of the applicability of the Commission's methods elsewhere must recognize the historical and social context in which the Commission's approach evolved. The issues and events, the nature of the region, the character and attitudes of the people, the degree of outside interest in the area, and other factors vary in different rural areas and can affect the success of a regional program.

TUG HILL TOWNS: The Region and Its People

THE TRADITIONAL TUG HILL AREA

As defined by the New York State Legislature, the Tug Hill region embraces portions of four counties, comprising more than 1.2 million acres. It includes parts of six recognized physiographic units: the Tug Hill Upland, Eastern Ontario Hills, Ontario Ridge and Swampland, Oneida Lake Plain, Black River Valley, and Mohawk Valley[1] (see Map 4). Only about 600 square miles of the largely forested summit area of the Tug Hill Upland is traditionally viewed as Tug Hill, however. This is often referred to in the Commission's work as the core area. One popular local writer described this isolated and sparsely populated area as "wild, wooded, beautiful—desolate, swampy, snowbound."[2]

goto p. 5

19

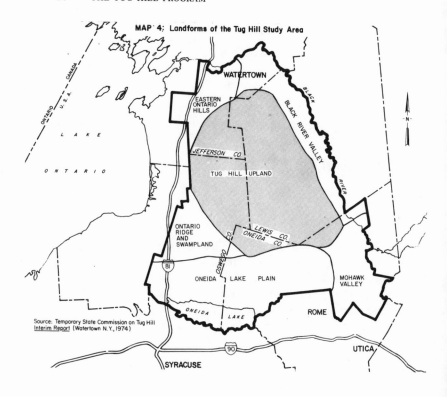

MAP 4; Landforms of the Tug Hill Study Area

Source: Temporary State Commission on Tug Hill
Interim Report (Watertown N.Y.,1974)

   The core area is almost entirely forest land. But the once-vigorous Tug Hill lumber industry logged almost all the commercially valuable timber. Due to soil, elevation, and climate conditions, the forest's annual growth rate is one of the lowest in New York State. Though some lumber is still harvested, the present forest is dominated by second growth hardwoods primarily of commercial value for pulpwood and, most recently, firewood.

   The hardwoods are mostly maple mixed with either elm and ash or beech and birch. About 10 percent of the forest cover is coniferous softwood, largely natural growths of spruce and fir, or plantations of red pine.

   The core area is isolated and contains a low, somewhat stable population surrounding a forested, uninhabited area at the center. No town has more than 1,800 residents. As one travels outward, the population progressively increases. These people have been termed individualistic and self-reliant. Many are descended from families that originally settled the area. One core area resident expressed it this way: "We drive a long way to our jobs. We wouldn't have stayed if we didn't like it here."[8]

THE STUDY AREA

State legislation creating the Tug Hill Commission set region boundaries which included thirty-nine towns and twenty villages in parts of Jefferson, Lewis, Oneida, and Oswego counties.

In New York, as in New England, "towns" are units of local government within counties. They encompass open country as well as areas of population concentration. Everyone in New York who lives outside a city or an Indian reservation lives in a town. Towns in New York frequently include within their boundaries separately incorporated units known as villages.

In many other states, "town" means a more heavily populated area similar to the village in New York State.

Approximately 81,500 people live in this study area, primarily in the northeastern and southern portions (see Map 3 and Table 2.1).[9]

TABLE 2.1

Tug Hill Towns in Relation to their Counties

County	Total County Population	Population of Tug Hill Area Towns	Percentage of County Population in Tug Hill Area	Total County Area (Acres)	Area of Tug Hill Towns (Acres)	Percentage of County Area in Tug Hill Area
Jefferson	88,508	15,811	17.9	812,038	187,634	23.1
Lewis	23,644	14,537	61.5	812,525	404,621	49.8
Oneida	273,037	32,887	12.0	727,027	359,104	49.4
Oswego	100,897	18,287	18.1	619,520	334,285	53.8
Total	486,086	81,521	16.8	2,971,110	1,285,644	43.3

Sources: State University of New York, College of Environmental Science and Forestry, *Resources of the Tug Hill Region* (Syracuse, N.Y.: February 1974); State of New York, *Manual for the Use of the Legislature* (Albany, N.Y.: 1975).

Lowville, the Lewis County seat, is one of the larger villages in the study area. Its 1970 population was 3,671. *Photograph courtesy of W. H. Kennedy, Jr.*

The primary centers of economic activity within this state-defined region are the predominantly agricultural northeastern rim and the largely residential southern rim (see Map 5). The major employment centers are located outside this thirty-nine-town area. There is little sense of overall regional identity, as expressed through regional organizations.[10] Overall, the area presents a fairly typical picture of rural America.

The Black River Valley lands of the northeastern portion of this region support many high quality dairy farms. Agricultural interests are powerful here, and there are no encroaching urban areas. Agriculture provides both an income and a way of life.[11]

More than half the region's people reside in the southern rim. Its

Dairy farming, particularly off the "hill," dominates the landscape and the economy. Jefferson, Lewis, and Oneida counties are consistently among the top milk producers in the New York-Pennsylvania milkshed. *Photograph courtesy of John L. Osinski.*

rapid growth is primarily residential, and activity focuses on nearby urban centers, such as Syracuse, Utica, and Rome. Population predictions show almost no growth for the core area in the next decade, and modest growth for the rest of the region. The exception is the towns on the region's southwestern edge, along Oneida Lake and near Rome and Utica, which are expected to grow faster.[12]

By most standards, the region's economy is not strong. In 1973, 43 percent of the region's employed residents commuted to jobs outside the region. Unemployment is high and incomes are low relative to the rest of New York State; yet residents do not consider poverty a problem.[13] The traditional economic bases are forestry and farming, including wood and food processing industries along the region's fringes.

MAP 5
Socioeconomic Subregions of the Tug Hill Study Area

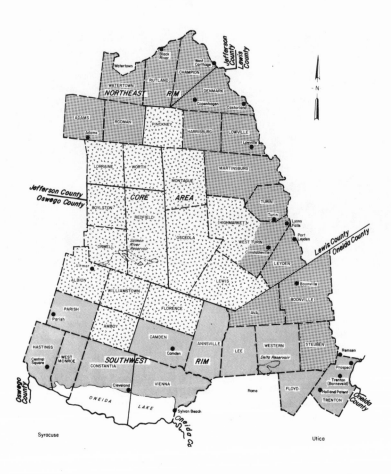

Source: State University of New York, College of Environmental Science and
Forestry, Resources of the Tug Hill Region (Syracuse, New York, Feb. 1974)

Logging is one economic base of the Tug Hill region. *Photograph courtesy of W. H. Kennedy, Jr.*

The logging industry has declined since its heyday around 1870. But with related industries, it still provides 15 percent of the region's jobs. While perhaps 775,000 acres (60 percent) of Tug Hill's extensive forests have some commercial potential, poor wood quality limits the future of this industry.[14]

Agriculture indirectly supports 25 percent of the area's total jobs. The percentage of land in agricultural use ranges from 1 percent in Redfield and Osceola, to 76 percent in Lowville. Marginal farmlands, particularly those immediately ringing the core area, have been reverting to forest or inactive uses since 1910. But dairy farms in the Black River Valley remain economically strong whether or not they are protected by agricultural districts.[15]

The Tug Hill region is changing character gradually. A major land use trend is the shift from agricultural to forest and inactive lands. One lifetime Boonville dairy farmer personalized the trend: "They say you should quit when feed hits 25 percent of your income; well, mine was up to 33 percent when I finally quit."

An increase in the amount of developed land since the 1960s has brought increasing land prices and property taxes to the area.[16] Many area residents note that these development pressures, strong in the early 1970s, have slowed recently. One area businessman described residential development as dying down in his formerly active town, and a core area resident observed a drop in construction of new camps. On the other hand, in the early part of 1980, inquiries were received on sizeable subdivisions in Lewis, Martinsburg, Turin, and Vienna. Thus development trends appear to be variable, over time as well as geographically.

SOCIAL ATTITUDES AND TOWN CAPABILITIES

Like many other rural people, Tug Hill residents resist planning and land use controls. Natural resource protection and home rule are two strongly expressed local concerns. At the same time, concern is also expressed for the economic health of these communities.[17] Two major outside threats are perceived: one is massive development resulting in change to their towns; the other is interference by the state.

Residents in many towns are suspicious of "new folks moving in with fancy ideas" and note what they perceive as changes for the worse in communities where this has occurred. One core area resident lamented, "It's not like it used to be." Another described his long ago move to the area but said, "I'd go somewhere else now."

Local political networks, until recently, were tightly knit, even closed. Tug Hill governments have, for the most part, had weak links to broader society and low influence with higher levels of government. This made them susceptible to strong outside influences.[18]

Local governments on Tug Hill are typical of many rural areas: part-time elected officials, with low financial, technical, and time resources for complex problem-solving. Home rule sentiment is so strong, and modern town administration so complicated, that one small town did not bother to file for federal revenue sharing funds in

MAP 6

County Governments and Regional Planning and Development Boards Serving the Tug Hill Area

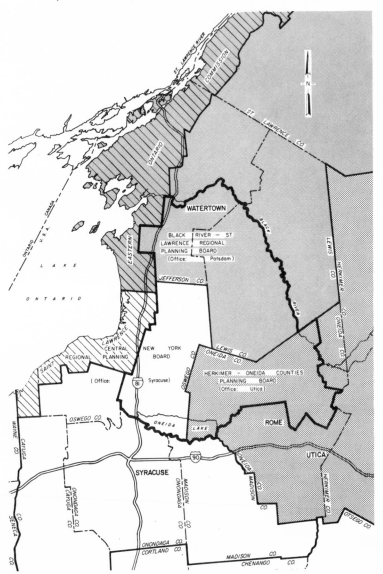

1974.[19] While towns on the area's suburban fringes are somewhat more sophisticated, they share many of the same problems and also have greater pressures on them. For some towns, experiencing no change for years, land use controls were not appropriate or needed. In these highly decentralized hamlets, even township land use planning is a step toward centralization in the minds of many residents.[20]

Nine of the thirty-nine towns and five of the villages had prepared master plans before the Commission's 1972 creation; few of these were ever adopted. Thirteen town and six village planning boards existed. Few zoning ordinances and subdivision regulations were in force, even on the region's fringes. In Lewis County particularly, local governments did not exercise their powers of land use control.[21] At the same time, these local governments were in general quite protective of their decision-making authority.

Prior to the Commission's creation, no governmental arrangements existed for considering this land area as one unit. But the area is served by a variety of higher-level government bodies. These include four county governments, three multicounty regional planning and development boards, two New York State Department of Environmental Conservation (DEC) regional offices, and three State Department of Health district offices (see Map 6). County governments and regional planning and development boards both tend to focus attention on their urban centers; Tug Hill is peripheral to their main concerns and geographically only one portion of their jurisdictions or administrative regions. All four counties have planning boards; three have staffed planning departments (Lewis County being the exception). County planning in these counties has not focused on supporting town planning for the more rural Tug Hill towns.

OUTSIDE ECONOMIC AND POLITICAL INTERESTS

Tug Hill has attracted little attention from statewide public interest groups. Private outside corporate interests have been active in the Tug Hill area for a long time, but their number is limited, compared with such areas as the Adirondacks or Catskills. The Niagara Mohawk Power Corporation owns the Salmon River Reservoir in Oswego County and much adjoining land. Georgia Pacific

The Georgia Pacific paper mill at Lyons Falls on the Black River employs about 300 people. *Photograph courtesy of John L. Osinski.*

Corporation, a timber company, is the largest private landowner, with more than 55,000 acres in two counties. It also operates a paper mill in Lyons Falls on the Black River and pays up to 16 percent of the property taxes in some Tug Hill towns.[22]

The late 1960s and early 1970s saw substantial land speculation by outsiders, primarily in the area's southeastern towns. Although the core area towns have long had nonresident landowners and small camp owners, the number of nonresident landowners and small-parcel seasonal residences increased in the late 1960s and early 1970s[23] (see Map 7). At Montague's 1977 public hearings on an interim zoning ordinance, seventy landowners attended though the town's population is only fifty-eight.

Only once in the last 15 years was a second home development of over 200 units proposed; it was later abandoned.[24] One Commission staff member described recent development activity as "picking away" at the region. But only a few small developments can alter the character of a rural town.

Many outsiders use Tug Hill for recreation. More than twenty fish and game clubs, some over fifty years old, lease core area land

MAP 7
Non–Resident Ownership as Percent of Privately Owned Land, 1974

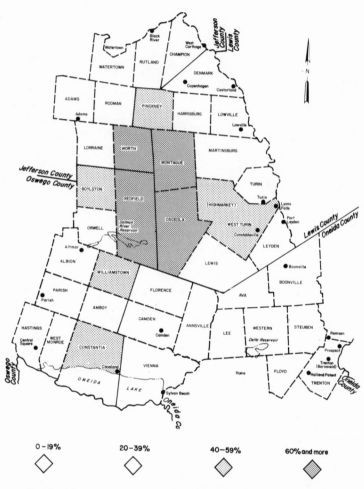

0 – 19%   20 – 39%   40 – 59%   60% and more

Source: Margaret Parsons and James Murray, <u>The Use, Value and Taxation of Tug Hill Lands</u> (Watertown, N.Y.: Temporary State Commission on Tug Hill, Sept. 1974).

20-39% shading should be for

Oswego County: Albion, Amboy, Orwell, Parish, West Monroe

Oneida County: Annsville, Boonville, Camden, Florence, Steuben, Vienna, Western

Jefferson County: Lorraine, Rodman

Lewis County: Harrisburg, Lewis, Martinsburg

Fish Creek is a fine stream for brook trout. *Photograph courtesy of W. H. Kennedy, Jr.*

to take advantage of the excellent hunting and fishing. These groups draw membership primarily from nearby urban areas. Club memberships are growing, along with recreational interest in Tug Hill. In addition to hunting and fishing, people from nearby urban areas are attracted to the area for snowmobiling, cross-country skiing, and other activities.[25] The Snow Ridge Resort in Turin also draws downhill skiers to the area. Twice in ten years Lewis County has been proposed as the site for a rock festival financed by outside interests. Residents' attitudes toward these outsiders can be summarized by one comment: "It's OK to have ski trails for city folk. But if I have to get somewhere I'm still going to snowmobile on them."

There is no extensive history of state-level legislative interest in the Tug Hill region, as in the Adirondacks or Catskills.[26] The region's forest resources, state-owned lands, water supply for surrounding areas, and its recreational use by both residents and outsiders have all been noted as legitimate state concerns.[27] Yet this interest has not, for the most part, been strongly expressed by state agencies, state officials, or statewide public interest groups. One state official commented that many individual state legislators still could not locate Tug Hill.

The New York State Department of Environmental Conservation (DEC) is the largest region landowner, managing approximately 140,000 acres of wildlife management and reforested lands, comprising 10.9 percent of the Commission's thirty-nine-town study area. This is much less than in the nearby Adirondacks, both in terms of the total number of acres of state lands and overall percentage. But in some towns state lands dominate; in the core towns of Montague and Florence, DEC owns 39 percent and 44 percent, respectively, of the land area.[28] Much of this land was acquired in the 1930s. State purchase of an additional 100,000 acres was considered as recently as 1972. With the exception of a few small parcels, these lands do not receive constitutional protection through State Forest Preserve status, as in the Catskills and Adirondacks.[29]

There is no evidence of strong concern for the area by influential individuals from other parts of the state. People from the New York City metropolitan area, who are influential in resource management decisions affecting the Adirondacks and Catskills, do not presently vacation in Tug Hill in large numbers. And statewide environmental groups have not voiced strong concern for the Tug Hill area.

THE STATE: Policies and Attitudes

New York has a long history of state interest in land use planning, with a wide range of experience in forming regional institutions to develop and implement land use policy.

State involvement in land use planning, especially for the state's rural areas, extends back to the first statewide land use planning report in 1926. Since then, state planning has moved in and out of favor, dependent on many factors, among them interest of the governor and availability of federal funding (see Table 2.2). The 1960s saw a burst of enthusiasm for statewide development planning,

TABLE 2.2

Key Individuals and Groups with an Interest in the Tug Hill Area

State Level:	Governors: Rockefeller, Wilson, Carey
	State Assembly
	State Senate
	Individual Assembly members and senators from outside the region
	N.Y.S. Dept. of Environmental Conservation
Regional Level:	Assembly members and senators representing the region
	Tug Hill Commission and individual commissioners
	Tug Hill Commission staff
	Three regional planning and development boards
County and Local Level:	Four County Boards of Supervisors or Legislatures
	Four County Planning Boards and three Departments
	Local town and village governing boards
	Cooperative Planning Boards and individual boards
	Agricultural interests
	Forestry interests
	Residents of core area
	Residents of southern rim
	Residents of northeastern rim
Outside Interests:	Georgia Pacific Corporation
	Niagara Mohawk Power Corporation
	Second home and summer camp owners
	Sportsmen's clubs in core area
	Outside land speculators
	Other tourists: hunters, fishermen, snowmobilers, hikers, park users

vigorously supported by then Governor Nelson A. Rockefeller. At the time of the Tug Hill Commission's creation in 1972, a regional environmental protection approach was popular.[30]

In the early 1960s, New York policy makers tended to view rural areas as potential sites for massive business and industrial expansion attracted by state programs. The 1964 landmark report, *Change/Challenge/Response,* by a new and strong State Office of Regional Development, suggested a policy of regional districts guided by a centralized state commission. A physical plan to prepare for predicted massive growth in the state was also proposed. This centralization of planning was strongly resisted by many nonmetropolitan local and county officials.

In 1966 the State Office of Planning Coordination (OPC) was created, becoming perhaps the strongest state planning organization in the country at that time. OPC's proposals were presented in *Development Plan I,* a physical land use plan for metropolitan New York State. The report's treatment of rural lands was oriented toward the perspective of people in metropolitan areas, emphasizing exceptional farmlands and natural resource preservation. The report was translated into proposed legislation in 1970, modeled on the American Law Institute's Model Land Development Code. It included state standards for land use planning and regulation, definition of areas of critical state concern, state review of local land use control proposals, and county development districts.[31] But opposition to OPC's stringent state land use control proposals, among other factors, led to a shift in strategy for state planning policy. OPC was subsequently dismantled in 1971.

The shift led to an emphasis on regionalism. A 1971 executive order divided the state into eleven comprehensive planning and development regions. Many of these multicounty regions were already served by regional planning boards created by counties in the 1960s. These boards were formed in response to federal financial assistance requirements and incentives, such as federal funds available for "701" planning programs from the Department of Housing and Urban Development. However, these regions, in keeping with the mood of the urban-dominated state legislature and the availability of federal funds for standard metropolitan statistical districts (SMSAs), were centered for the most part around metropolitan rather than rural regions. As noted, the Tug Hill area lies within the jurisdictions of three of these boards.[32]

Caught in the prevailing national mood of the early 1970s, New York State passed environmental legislation designed to regulate land uses in certain critical natural areas by land type, such as wetlands and flood plains. A stringent version of the federal National

Environmental Policy Act, the 1975 State Environmental Quality Review Act (SEQRA), extended environmental impact statement requirements even to local government activities.[33]

Other actions were taken to improve state environmental management. For example, in 1970, several programs were consolidated to create DEC, which now administers much of the state's land use legislation affecting natural resource protection. A $1.2 million bond issue for environmental protection was passed in 1972 by state voters. And local conservation advisory commissions were promoted for local governments.[34] In addition, state and national environmental groups combined to provide a strong environmental lobby in the state capital.

New York State has also looked to regional responses to rural land use issues. In the past fifteen years it has formed several independent agencies or study commissions to focus on rural regions "of statewide concern" and develop measures to protect and enhance the natural and socioeconomic resources of these areas. Only one of these, the Temporary Study Commission on the Future of the Adirondacks, was appointed by the governor; the others were legislative creations.

In 1965 a Hudson River Valley Commission was granted development review powers along the Hudson River. It was followed in 1969 by the St. Lawrence-Eastern Ontario Commission (SLEOC), to encourage control of shoreline development, erosion, and flooding problems. The 1968 Temporary Study Commission on the Future of the Adirondacks led to formation of the Adirondack Park Agency (APA) in 1971, which was charged with developing a regional land use plan and given regulatory powers to implement it. A study commission for the Catskill Mountains was also created in 1971.[35]

The results of these programs, and local reaction to them, has varied. Of these agencies, only the Adirondack Park Agency was given regulatory powers to implement a regional plan. The plan was enacted by the state legislature in 1973 and became effective in August of that year. A similar permanent regional agency proposed for the Catskills failed to gain legislative approval. The Hudson River Valley Commission staff was disbanded in 1971, although the Commission itself remained legally in existence until 1980. SLEOC has continued to function as a shoreline management agency. Achievement of the goals set forth for these commissions had been heavily dependent on the degree of success in stimulating and fostering local support.[36]

The prevailing mood in Albany in 1972 was environmentally oriented, with regionalism, environmental protection regulation, and land use planning emerging as solutions offered by many to common problems of rural areas. The state legislature was at that time liberal, urban-dominated, free-spending, and influenced by a strong governor. New York State and many of its influential thinkers were in the forefront of national trends involving state action on land use and environmental issues. This mind set not only influenced the actual formation of a regional study commission for Tug Hill, but was reflected, to an extent, in what the commissioners thought they were expected to accomplish.

THE COMMISSION'S EARLY HISTORY

THE COMMISSION'S CREATION

Concern among a few influential individuals and groups from the area's fringes, some with connections outside the area, prompted the Commission's creation. The late state assembly member, Edward F. Crawford, representing Oswego County, was the major force behind the Commission's creation. Two crisis events in the early 1970s stimulated a local consciousness concerning the nature and importance of Tug Hill as a natural resource. These events were proposals for a rock festival in Lewis County and a major second home development in Lewis and Oswego counties (see Table 2.3).

Reaction in Lewis County to a proposed 1970 rock festival for 100,000 participants, financed by a New York City company, was extreme. The plans drew hostility from the Lewis County Board of Legislators, the County Farm Bureau, the County Chamber of Commerce, and residents. A massive influx of outsiders was seen as costing the county a great deal in medical, water, police, transportation on two parcels of Georgia-Pacific core area forest land. These residents of Harrisburg, where the festival was to be held, at first welcomed it, then changed as opposition mounted. The festival was cancelled after a threatened lawsuit by Lewis County and passage of

TABLE 2.3

Chronology of the Tug Hill Commission

1970	June	Rock festival is proposed for Lewis County
1971	July	Horizon takes option on 55,000 acres of Tug Hill land
1972	May 4	State legislature passes bill to create Temporary State Commission on Tug Hill
	June 8	Governor signs bill creating Tug Hill Commission
1973	March	Nine commissioners are appointed
	May	State legislature expands study boundaries to include eleven more towns
	October	Commission hires executive director
1974	February	SUNY Forestry team completes natural resources inventory
	March 31	Commission submits Interim Report
	Feb.–May	Commission holds eight public forums; 1,500 attend
	October	Nine core area towns form the Cooperative Tug Hill Planning Board
1975	February	Commission begins pilot local government technical assistance program
	March	Commission issues Preliminary Findings and Recommendations
	June	Commission holds eight public forums on preliminary findings; 300 attend
	November	Commission issues major revisions in preliminary findings
1976	February	Commission issues final report to state
	May	Five municipalities form Salmon Rivers Cooperative Planning Board
	September	Cooperative Tug Hill Planning Board completes resource management plan
1977	May	Four towns form North Shore Cooperative Planning Board
	June	Cooperative Tug Hill Planning Board adopts model Rural Development Code
	September	Commission resolves to disband by March 31, 1981
	November	Three towns form Jefferson County Snowbelt Cooperative Planning Board
1978	August	Four towns form Northeast Oneida Planning Board
1979	June	Salmon Rivers Cooperative Planning Board completes comprehensive plan
1979	November	Commission holds two workshops on its phase-out; 125 attend
1981	March 31	Temporary Commission's planned expiration date

a county law regulating large gatherings.[37] But as much uproar as the festival caused, by the next year this sense of crisis had dissipated.

Another sense of crisis developed among a number of concerned individuals in reaction to the Horizon Corporation's $6 million option on two parcels of Georgia Pacific core area forest land. These parcels were one of 52,000 acres in the six Lewis County towns, and one of 11,000 acres in Redfield, Oswego County.[38] The option was first publicized in late August 1971, though company representatives had met with county planners to discuss the Oswego lands at least two months earlier.

Georgia Pacific apparently was quietly trying to sell this land for some time before the Horizon option was taken. For example, a state forester observed what he termed extensive "liquidation cuttings" on company lands in the 1960s. Feasibility studies of possible development were also prepared, financed by the company.[39]

For weeks after the announcement, there was little visible reaction to the proposed development. Then opposition suddenly emerged through the efforts of the assembly member Crawford.

Reaction in Lewis County was not widespread or negative. The proposed development appealed to some county leaders by utilizing a remote corner of the county. The assembly member then representing Jefferson and Lewis counties did not react strongly to the Horizon proposal or actively try to stop it.

A vague concern was prevalent among some residents, hunting club members, and farmers on the fringes of the core area. But only a few people throughout the area were outspoken in their objections and moved to some form of action. This was apparently centered in Oswego County, although some business leaders in the Boonville area also privately expressed reservations.

Objections to Horizon's proposal were raised by the Southeastern Oswego County Environmental Tactical Society (SOCETS), a small citizen group led by Professor Richard Mark of the State University of New York, College of Environmental Science and Forestry; a few influential local Oswego County political leaders; at least one logger and sawmill owner; members of a major hunting club that leased Georgia Pacific land; and the regional office of DEC. Concerns centered on negative environmental impacts of the proposal, loss of the area's unique wild character, and local governments becoming overwhelmed by a massive development. In addition,

SOCETS' interests included wildlife, forest management, and watershed protection for the core area. DEC managed nearby state lands and was then considering additional land purchases.

These concerns were expressed to assembly member Crawford, primarily after rumors of Oswego County development began. Crawford raised the Horizon issue in the local media. When Horizon dropped its option and decided the land was not suitable for such use, publicity about possible threats to the core area continued. Crawford continued his search for some form of action, explaining, "The fact that this came so close to happening should encourage all those persons who wish to preserve the wilderness quality of that area to get busy to get a cloak of protection for it."[40]

But Crawford had yet to decide on a strategy to protect Tug Hill. DEC was consulted about possible actions. The idea of a study commission apparently came from an informal meeting of Crawford, SOCETS, and an Adirondack Park Agency board member, Peter Paine. Called in to discuss a possible APA study or extension of the Adirondack Park to include Tug Hill, Paine instead suggested a separate study commission to consider future regional responses to development pressures.[41]

Crawford translated this into action by a letter that fall to state legislative leaders outlining the proposed temporary study commission. Tug Hill area legislators agreed to cosponsor a bill, particularly Senator Douglas H. Barclay, a long-term Republican and the major force behind SLEOC, another state regional commission.[42] A short-term study commission appeared as a nonthreatening and reasonable suggestion; the bill's broad charge allowed many possibilities. Aid in drafting the bill was received from both DEC and SOCETS president Richard Mark.

The proposed commission did not spark strong reaction within the Tug Hill area, despite the potential for strong hostility to state action. Supporting letters were received from Jefferson and Oneida counties, the Boonville Chamber of Commerce, and several individual towns; each county legislature adopted a supporting resolution. This indicated a wait-and-see attitude, however, rather than outright enthusiasm. Two negative comments were received, from the Herkimer-Oneida Comprehensive Planning Board concerning duplication of existing planning efforts, and from the Lewis County Chamber of Commerce regarding the study region's boundaries.

Yet significantly, many local and even county political leaders claim they were not consulted about either the usefulness of a study commission or its passage by the state legislature. One knowledgeable Lewis County respondent described the Tug Hill Commission's formation as taking place "behind an iron curtain in Oswego County." For the most part, area residents were unaware of the Commission's existence until it held public forums in 1974. This potential local opposition was one early factor the Commission had to deal with.

At the state level, DEC strongly supported the bill, but the State Office of Planning Services commented unfavorably about overlapping planning services.[43] Statewide environmental groups and other public interest groups that might normally support such a regional commission were silent, as were groups that might oppose it, such as the New York State Farm Bureau. Despite state land ownership in the core area, the Commission's creation was more a political favor to Crawford than a reflection of strong state concern for the region.

The bill easily and quickly passed both Republican-dominated houses by large margins, arousing no significant debate.[44] Thus the Tug Hill Commission began its operation with strong support from a select few, with questionable state-level support, and with potential opposition from many local residents.

DEFINING TUG HILL

Defining the boundaries of the Tug Hill study region was not a simple task. After several alterations, the study region encompasses a much larger area than is traditionally known as Tug Hill. This broad definition affected both the Commission's approach and the success of its efforts. The lack of a strong regional identity among many area residents became a hindrance to acceptance of standard regional planning methods.

The 1972 legislation included twenty-seven towns in the study region, but this boundary was altered several times in 1973 and 1974.[45] The region was expanded considerably, adding towns along the eastern and western fringes, while four towns bordering Lake Ontario were removed (see Map 8). After this, some agreement appears to have been reached, for no further boundary changes

MAP 8
Boundary Changes in the Tug Hill Study Area

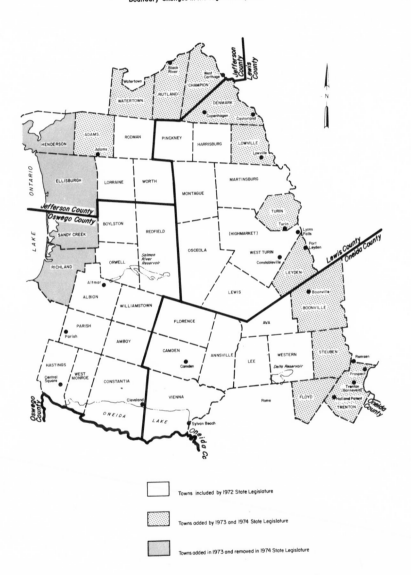

Towns included by 1972 State Legislature

Towns added by 1973 and 1974 State Legislature

Towns added in 1973 and removed in 1974 State Legislature

occurred.[46] The resulting study area of thirty-nine towns and twenty villages remains unchanged.

There had been no previous political recognition of the Tug Hill area and no evidence of regional cohesion. Many perceptions existed as to what constituted the Tug Hill region. Most agreed on the sparsely populated core area and its natural resource, the forest. Outside this central area, disagreement exists as to where Tug Hill is. One writer noted in 1967 that "none of the settlements around or even on the plateau will concede that they are part of Tug Hill. Copenhagen, Lowville, Martinsburg, Turin, Constableville, West Leyden, Redfield, Pulaski, Adams or Watertown are definitely not Tug Hill"[47] (see Map 9).

The 1972 boundaries were drawn, almost literally overnight, by Professor Mark. In keeping with his scientific training and what he saw as the natural resource protection focus of the bill, he used soil types, elevation, forest cover, physiography, and other natural science criteria to define Tug Hill. He then included all towns that met these criteria as part of Tug Hill.[48] Thus the 1972 bill represented a natural resource definition of Tug Hill.

As Mark later put it, "The scientific criteria didn't go over." Senator Barclay recalls that some towns wanted out, not perceiving their physical relationship to Tug Hill, or that they had common interests with other Tug Hill towns on the strength of this factor alone. At the same time, others wanted to be included for possible state assistance. Some Lewis County officials were angered that certain towns were left out, as they felt that most of Tug Hill is in Lewis County. In reaction to this, the dominant sentiment became to add as many towns as possible.

By increasing the number of fringe towns, the traditionally recognized Tug Hill (or core area) became obscured in a larger area. This reduced the potential for social identification with the area in which the Commission was directed to work. But the population served by the Commission, and thus the rationale for state-level involvement, increased.

Some protest, both local and regional, developed over the region's boundaries. The four Lake Ontario shoreline towns, which were also part of the St. Lawrence-Eastern Ontario Commission's (SLEOC) jurisdiction, were removed at SLEOC's request to reduce jurisdictional overlap. In 1973 the towns of Watertown and Cham-

MAP 9
Tug Hill As A Social Territory: Twentieth-Century View

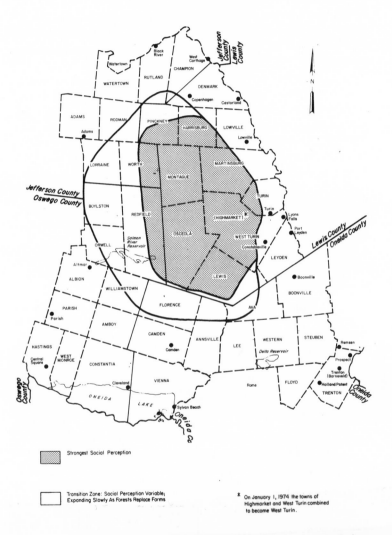

Strongest Social Perception

Transition Zone: Social Perception Variable;
Expanding Slowly As Forests Replace Farms

* On January 1, 1974 the towns of
Highmarket and West Turin combined
to become West Turin.

Source: Lyle S. Raymond, Jr., "Tug Hill: Defining
a Meaningful Area for Regional Development," Proceedings of the Northern New York–Lake Champlain
Environmental Conference (Chazy, N.Y.: Institute
for Man and His Environment, 1974).

pion requested removal from the region, though Champion was more vocal in its protest. Champion felt no identity with Tug Hill and declared that its problems could be treated alone, without state interference. A long-term town board member stated, "We weren't ever in Tug Hill, not really." Further, the Champion town board was offended that it was not consulted about joining the area in the first place.[49]

The present Tug Hill study region population density is nearly twice that of the Adirondack Park, although the density of the sixteen core area towns is one-fourth that of the total study region. Expansion of the study region boundaries increased the importance of local political forces and of local government opinion in the more populous peripheral towns which became a strong factor influencing the Commission's work.

THE COMMISSION'S FIRST YEARS

Creation of the Temporary State Commission on Tug Hill did not stem from a grass roots effort to preserve Tug Hill. Development of a broader local political support base for its activities was undertaken by the Commission after its formation. This task was aided by the Commission's broad charge, which allowed much flexibility in activities and policy formation. This charge included the study of:

> the conservation and development of the natural resources of the region, notably, the flora, fauna, scenic beauty and environmental purity; the strengthening of cultural resources, social organizations, economy and general well-being of the rural communities and the development of measures by which the region may draw strength from neighboring areas, but at the same time protecting itself from unplanned population growth. Also studied should be the necessity of strengthening policy regarding management, acquisition and use of public land; the development of controls for highways, public buildings and utilities; the measures to be taken by local governments to assure that the development of private lands is consistent with the long-range plans.[50]

Nine commissioners were appointed in March 1973, three each by the governor, senate temporary president, and assembly Speaker.

This group made several important early decisions that affected later events and Commission policies, among them selecting an executive director and holding public forums as one of their first public activities. The direction expected of the Commission was not clear from state legislation or other commissions' examples, so they set their own. Policy recommendations in the Commission's mandated 1976 report to the state legislature reflected primarily local concerns, an emphasis that continues in present programs.

While legislation required only three of the nine commissioners to be region residents, all but assembly member Crawford were. Crawford was elected to chair the Commission, and monthly meetings began in April 1973. They selected Watertown, near the Tug Hill region, as their headquarters. A factor in this decision was the availability of office space in a new State Office Building.

The Commission was originally mandated to report back to the legislature and governor by March 31, 1973. As this was not possible, the legislature extended this date twice, first to March 1974, then to March 1975.[51] Subsequent extensions have been obtained through appropriations in annual state budget bills rather than specific legislation.

The Commission was given a broad charge, but not regional authority. Its first newsletter explained that the charge "covers all factors affecting the quality of life—all life—in and around the Tug Hill plateau."[52] Unsure of the role of the Commission, one commissioner said, "I don't know how to reconcile the two states of mind we keep hearing. On one hand, people want us to leave them alone to control their own land, yet they want the land preserved the way it is. If someone can tell me how to do both, I'll be very grateful."[53]

Following the example of the Temporary State Commissions on the Adirondacks and Catskills, one of the group's first actions was to contract for a natural resource inventory of Tug Hill by the SUNY College of Environmental Science and Forestry at Syracuse, to provide an information base for their decisions.[54] Other detailed studies, some with consultants, followed up on specific issues raised by the inventory. This regionwide natural resource data base simplified later planning efforts.

In October 1973, the Commission selected an engineer with community development experience for the position of executive director. The next two professional staff members, a natural resource

Tug Hill public forums in Lorraine (above) and in West Leyden (right). *Photographs courtesy of W. H. Kennedy, Jr.*

planner and community participation coordinator, were added seven and a half months later. The new director's attitude is reflected in his article in the Commission's first newsletter, directed at Tug Hill residents: "I look forward to the work ahead because it presents a chance to work on a different approach to this sometimes controversial process called 'planning'. . . . Land like that on the Tug Hill plateau is becoming too rare today to expect that it will be kept natural . . . without some sort of guiding policy. I strongly believe that such policy can be developed by the people if they are given sufficient facts to look ahead and see future alternatives."[55]

With the aid of New York State Cooperative Extension and community leaders throughout the Tug Hill area, the Commission planned a series of eight public forums in early 1974 to answer questions and hear citizen concerns (see Table 2.4). Steering committees to plan these forums involved about 100 community leaders. These forums were held well before any policy recommendations were agreed upon.

With these forums, the Commission hoped to open lines of communication with area residents, landowners, and members of diverse interest groups.[56] Advertisements for the forums billed their

purpose as "to hear what citizens would like the future of Tug Hill to be. . . . Through these forums we hope to involve the people of the Tug Hill region from the beginning in the decision-making process."[57] In addition, guidance was sought as to the Commission's role. The Commission later used the information obtained from these forums to develop eight basic goals for the Tug Hill area.

By the time of the forums, many local citizens and governments saw the Commission as more of a threat than development pressures. One Adams resident at the first forum was applauded for saying, "I wish the Tug Hill Commission would say to the state, keep out of Tug Hill and we'll call you if we want you."[58] The forums attracted a large turnout of fifteen hundred people, including area interest groups and many local political leaders. A substantial range of opin-

TABLE 2.4

Tug Hill Commission Public Forums

1974	Attendance
2/27 Lorraine, Jefferson County	200
3/07 Watertown Center, Jefferson County	120
3/28 Lowville, Lewis County	500
4/04 West Leyden, Lewis County	320
4/29 Central Square, Oswego County	60
5/07 Holland Patent, Oneida County	50
5/13 Redfield, Oswego County	225
5/16 Camden, Oneida County	50
	1,505
1975	
6/09 Watertown Center, Jefferson County	60
6/12 Camden, Oneida County	20
6/16 West Leyden, Lewis County	40
6/19 Holland Patent, Oneida County	30
6/23 Parish, Oswego County	30
6/25 Lowville, Lewis County	30
6/27 Redfield, Oswego County	40
6/30 Lorraine, Jefferson County	50
	300

Sources: Tug Hill Commission; Watertown *Daily Times*.

ion, from outright hostility to a more reasoned wait-and-see acceptance, was expressed over the course of the forums. Although many issues were raised, discussion kept returning to land use issues and controls.[59]

The Commission's Interim Report, delivered to the governor and state legislature on March 31, 1974, summarized the natural resource inventory findings, introduced the Commission, and highlighted responses at the first four public forums.[60] Preliminary findings, delivered in March 1975, were prepared jointly by staff and Commission members, with informal advice from affected local in-

TABLE 2.5

The Commission's Eight Goals

1. Keep Tug Hill the way it is.
2. Maintain a healthy economy.
3. Maintain the present high quality of Tug Hill air.
4. Protect Tug Hill's watershed and unique areas for enjoyment and utilization.
5. Maintain agriculture as a way of life and as one of the mainstays of the economy.
6. Maintain Tug Hill forests for timber, wildlife, and recreation.
7. Maintain the recreational values of Tug Hill while providing economic benefits to those who live here now.
8. Preserve "home rule" while keeping the cost of government (taxes) in line.

terest groups such as farm bureaus and chambers of commerce. The findings were organized around the eight region goals that the commissioners interpreted from comments at the first public forums[61] (see Table 2.5).

After several months of local and state review, including eight more public forums, only two major changes were made. These changes were in recommendations that received the most local criticism, the land use planning program and stream protection under the State Wild, Scenic, and Recreational Rivers Act.[62] In March 1976, the Commission presented the governor and the legislature with a report containing fifty-six recommendations for state and local action. This report was titled *The Tug Hill Region: Preparing for the Future.*[63]

The fifty-six recommendations emphasized the role of local government in handling most area issues, concluding that "local government can direct effectively the future of Tug Hill—if the necessary support is provided."[64] That statement became a cornerstone of the Commission's philosophy, setting the overall tone and approach for subsequent Commission programs.

3 The Tug Hill Commission: Its Program

EVOLUTION OF THE COMMISSION'S APPROACH

THE TUG HILL COMMISSION has changed much over its eight-year existence, in approach, focus, and activities, although a strong local orientation has remained a common theme. Beginning its work as a temporary study commission emphasizing areawide policy development for natural resource protection and regional land use planning, it now focuses its energies on action programs for local government assistance and embraces much more than traditional land use planning. Its current program, as of March 1980, combining elements of several conventional methods, contrasts with the approaches of other similar regional commissions.

The Commission presently describes itself as "testing an approach for developing and implementing land use and natural resource policy for a region by starting at the local level."[1] Three program areas support this "experiment in rural land use policy": developing land use planning and controls from the local level up through intertown cooperation; providing a wide range of guidance and technical assistance to local government upon request; and acting as a sponsor for community education efforts. The Commission emphasizes the input, cooperation, and participation of local governments and area residents, both in its role as a regional advocate to the state and in its land use planning and local government assistance programs. This has been taken one step further, by fostering decision-making on land use issues by the local governments themselves. Underlying all the Commission's decisions to date is a firm belief in home rule and the ability of people of a rural area to decide for themselves.

Nevertheless, the Tug Hill Commission is not a local agency. It has responsibilities to the state and a regional mission. Within this, however, the Commission sees itself as a strong advocate of local government and of the Tug Hill area. In its 1976 report, it professed the faith that, "When facts were made available, town and village planning boards working together would usually make decisions for the good of the area as a whole."[2]

This approach has evolved over the years. Major elements of the Commission's current program were not part of its original charge or original activities. Although the Commission's charter permits attention to many issues, its early focus was primarily on land use planning, rather than economic development or other issues. This focus dates back to the first public forums in 1974, where discussion kept returning to planning and controls, even though many other regional issues were voiced as well.[3] It was also a reflection of then common assumptions about rural areas and how to solve their problems and what the commissioners felt was expected of this and other state-created regional commissions.

Initially, the Commission also defined the issues of the Tug Hill area primarily in natural resource terms. Thus the Commission's original goal of "Keep Tug Hill the Way It Is" was pursued primarily by recommendations aimed at protecting the region's natural resources. Action programs in economic development were not emphasized, though the Commission did sponsor research on the area's economy. This focus on the issues has changed somewhat, as the Commission has moved away from a view of its role as a region policy maker to one of assisting area local governments.

The present highly flexible and locally oriented planning approach evolved as the Commission continued to try out proposals in the Tug Hill area. The Commission's early areawide land use planning recommendations gradually gave way to a town-level–up approach, involving formation of intertown "cooperative" planning boards among groups of towns. This evolution resulted largely from a successful early experiment in which the Cooperative Tug Hill Planning Board (CTHPB) was formed by officials from nine core area towns in four different counties in October 1974. This is described in more detail later (see Table 3.1).

TABLE 3.1

Summary of Tug Hill Commission's Recommendations
February 1976

---

1. Prepare a regional plan and implementing mechanism from town and subregional plans and actions.

2. Support economic development of forestry, agriculture, and related industries.

3. Study acid precipitation and its sources.

4. Protect streams, gorges, and wetlands through local government action.

5. Stabilize agricultural lands through local planning, tax reform, and agricultural districts.

6. Maintain forest multiple use through local planning, tax reform, and forest management programs.

7. Develop low intensity recreational trails, while guarding landowner interests.

8. Reform state and private property tax policies.

9. Provide technical and financial assistance to local government.

Source: Temporary State Commission on Tug Hill, *The Tug Hill Region—Preparing for the Future* (Watertown, N.Y.: February 1976), p. 6.

Another factor in changing the Commission's approach was strong negative reaction within the Tug Hill area, in at least two instances during development of the Commission's 1976 report, to major proposals for regional resource protection and planning. One of these involved use of the state's Wild, Scenic and Recreational Rivers Act to protect streams in the area. This method was opposed by the CTHPB, farm interests, and the Georgia Pacific Corporation. The Commission also proposed a regional land use planning program, building a regional plan from mandated local plans and land use controls developed by joint town planning boards with Commission technical assistance. These joint boards were to be represented on a Tug Hill regional council.[4] The CTHPB, among others, rejected this proposal as a threat to local control, and the Commission reconsidered. By early 1977, the Commission was describing its land use planning process as "incremental and evolutionary," rather than regional, and had dropped the idea of one formal planning model that could be applied to all Tug Hill communities.[5]

Besides local reaction, advice from other groups with community development experience also influenced the Commission's approach. In addition to the negative example of the Adirondack Park Agency, the commissioners observed the facilitative approach of Cooperative Extension to community development in other parts of rural New York State. Further, a 1974 northeast regional conference on rural land use policy, held when the Commission was forming its ideas about land use planning, provided interchange with many other groups.[6]

The Commission does not now promote regional planning in the usual sense. Rather, staff members see planning as an educational process, not just following a cookbook approach to produce goals or a neat package of regulatory products. The Commission describes its reliance on cooperative, voluntary, local decision-making as an alternative to other regional planning methods.[7] Local consensus, not zoning and regulation, is said to be the end of this highly flexible process. While towns may cooperate in developing intertown subregional plans, their involvement is entirely voluntary, and there will be no formal regional plan. Technical expertise is provided to advise and assist local governments, not decide for them.

The Commission has emphasized more and more the importance of assisting local governments in other areas besides planning. In September 1979, the director stated: "We in fact believe that planning is only one function of local government and have directed our efforts to finding and testing ways to build total capability for local governance. We see ourselves, then, not primarily as a rural land use program, but as an experiment in facilitation of effective local government."[8] All of this is oriented to, in the words of one staff member, "the one unique thing we do: we pin down their needs, and they make the choices."

THE COMMISSION'S PROGRAM

Components of the Commission's current program, as outlined recently by the Commission director, include: local planning assistance; training and technical assistance to local officials; assistance with community organization and communications; public information and education programs; and providing information on issues that affect the whole area. A primary goal in these efforts is to build local independence from the Commission.[9]

LOCAL PLANNING ASSISTANCE

Local planning assistance from the Commission is channeled primarily through cooperative town planning boards, composed of groupings of several towns which have elected to undertake planning as a joint effort. This assistance has been delivered without formal strings attached, and in many cases at minimal or no cost to the communities. Participation is voluntary, though the Commission may try to persuade towns to become involved.

It is important to note that the technical side of planning assistance is buttressed by other components of the Commission's program.

Once a cooperative town planning board is formed with the Commission's assistance, the Commission continues to provide both planning and community organizational help to organize the process and to fully involve the community. Besides strengthening local capabilities, technical assistance and citizen education efforts are designed to build long-term understanding of local cooperative planning and to gain immediate support for Commission planning efforts. The Cooperative Tug Hill Planning Board (CTHPB) was the first cooperative board to be organized. The Commission's planning assistance program was developed while working with this board and thus is illustrative of the Commission's approach.[10]

With substantial technical assistance from the Commission staff, the CTHPB undertook community and natural resource inventories, drafted a natural resource management plan, and prepared a model land development code.[11] Many diverse regulations, such as subdivision and zoning, that are usually dealt with separately with conventional approaches, are included in this code. In this several-step planning process, background information on the area was presented to CTHPB members. Commission staff organized board members' statements of individual town goals, and together they developed a joint natural resource plan and resource goals.

Similar versions of the model rural development code had been adopted by seven of the towns as of April 1980. The remaining two had held public hearings on the issue in 1978, but showed no signs that they would adopt the code soon. Five towns have banded together, in an unusual exercise of joint municipal authority, to implement and enforce the code through an intermunicipal agreement. The Commission has called this joint exercise of power "the most important step in welding together the cooperative program."[12]

The Commission is no longer extensively involved in CTHPB activities or those of its member towns, excepting two potential new members, Lewis and Turin. But the success of initial planning assistance efforts developed with the CTHPB launched the Commission into similar assistance programs with another seventeen towns and five villages, organized into four additional cooperative planning boards. Recently, it has also provided planning assistance to individual towns for specific regulatory issues, such as trailer ordinances.

The other four cooperative planning boards differ in both purposes and activities from the original board. There is presently no one model of how planning is conducted for these boards. None has adopted a model local land use regulation. One board has completed a draft comprehensive development plan, and two others have begun their own form of planning activity. Yet, primarily through Commission action, an additional twenty-two individual town and village planning boards have formed, covering much of the Tug Hill land area. Comprehensive plans have been completed by thirteen towns and villages and are being prepared by twelve more. Part of this increased interest in planning activities is a result of the Commission providing assistance not just with the planning process, but with organization, technical information, and other aspects of local land use management (see Table 3.2).

TRAINING AND TECHNICAL ASSISTANCE TO LOCAL OFFICIALS

The Tug Hill Commission also provides individualized assistance to local officials on a wide variety of subjects related to the operation of rural local government.

A pilot technical assistance program began in February 1975, after Commission staff discovered a need for assistance to Tug Hill

TABLE 3.2

The Cooperative Planning Process for the CTHPB

1. Local expression of interest.
2. Joint information session by the commission; hosted by one of towns.
3. Individual town planning board formation and appointment of two representatives per town to cooperative planning board.
4. Cooperative work program development.
5. Community coordinator hired with grant funds.
6. Community inventories of individual towns: natural resources, existing land use, land capabilities, economic studies, transportation, public services, and other.
7. Citizen survey.
8. Individual town goals and objectives formulation, followed by integrating these at cooperative level.
9. Natural and man-made limitations maps prepared.
10. Design of sketch maps and plans individually, following by combination of individual sketch maps and plans for cooperative board.
11. Draft of cooperative Resource Management Plan.
12. Cooperative consideration of implementation alternatives, and cooperative preparation of draft rural development code.
13. Individual town review and adoption of Rural Development Code.
14. Cooperative administration and enforcement through intermunicipal agreement.

communities in matters besides land use planning. Its purpose was to "assist local government officials in serving the people of the region."[13] A Commission staff member acted as a referral service to answer local government officials' information requests on a wide range of subjects, such as budgeting, road specifications, snowmobile control, and water supply. This coordinator obtained answers from the appropriate state or county agency. While the major users of this first service were core area towns and the CTHPB, numerous requests were received from towns outside the core area.[14]

The program was expanded in 1977 with federal Inter-

Seminar for clerks of towns in the Salmon Rivers and North Shore cooperative planning areas.

governmental Personnel Act (IPA) funds channeled through the New York Department of State (DOS).[15] Local officials from the nine core towns received direct individual assistance with local government management problems from visits of a "circuit rider." The "circuit rider," by regular visits to local officials, served as a personal link between them and outside resources. The formal technical assistance program to fulfill information requests continued.

In addition, through the IPA grant, four training sessions were held for local clerks, supervisors, and town board members on such topics as fiscal responsibilities, decision-making, taking effective minutes, responsibilities of various town officials, and legal aspects of these positions. Training sessions were often prepared with the help of the DOS's Community Affairs Division and adapted partly from packaged courses. But they were geared to specific problems voiced by officials in these small rural towns. The four training sessions were evaluated by those attending. These remarks by nearly fifty local officials were highly favorable, in terms of the usefulness of the information and how it was presented.[16]

Presently, the Commission provides a range of training programs and information services for officials in all thirty-nine towns of the Tug Hill area. More than 700 separate requests were logged by January 1980. About one-fifth concerned local finances; other popular topics included management, legal advice, planning, and zoning. Special information programs, such as those on administering local environmental quality review and wetlands laws, address frequently asked questions.

Requests are received from local planning boards, cooperative boards, town clerks, and town and village boards. Heaviest users of the technical assistance program are the CTHPB and the towns of Osceola, Pinckney, Lorraine, and Constantia (since 1975), Orwell (since 1976), and Adams, West Monroe, and Vienna (since 1978); all are cooperative board members. Cooperative boards or their member towns filed more than 600 of the 700 requests to January 1980. Only three towns and seven villages in the Commission's region have never contacted the Commission, and nine other municipalities have sought assistance just once.

The Commission also, on occasion, identifies and publicizes programs of importance to local governments. For example, in 1977 the Commission notified area local governments of federal money available through the new Public Employment Project Program (now CETA) and helped interested officials meet the tight deadline for submitting proposals to their county. The result: seventeen out of twenty-five proposals submitted by thirteen towns and villages were funded for a total of $124,000.[17] In a similar promotion, the Commission encouraged adoption of local wetlands ordinances to implement the state Freshwater Wetlands Act ahead of the 1976 deadline for local adoption in thirty-nine of the forty-four municipalities affected.[18]

A local technical assistance program covering topics other than planning is somewhat unusual for most regional commissions. Some individual commissioners have expressed reservations about the need of local governments for such assistance and the role of a commission with regional scope in providing it. Yet, this program is seen by those who use it as perhaps the most crucial service the Commission provides. And the Commission staff thoroughly supports the need for this program. The Commission's community participation coordinator feels that providing technical assistance to local governments is the key to being able to do the rest, by building a working relationship with them.

The Commission is now experimenting with transfer of its technical assistance program to other agencies. A second IPA grant to the Commission established an Office of Town and Village Assistance in the fall of 1979 for Oneida County, through the county Cooperative Extension office. This office in Rome, N.Y., staffed by a program coordinator, provides technical assistance on individual questions, "circuit rider" outreach services to communities, and training sessions for local officials throughout Oneida County.[19]

PUBLIC INFORMATION PROGRAMS

Citizen information and education have all along been implicit goals of the Commission's activities. From the first public forums drawing fifteen hundred people to present extensive public education programs, the Commission has demonstrated that it considers citizen involvement to be a significant aspect of its work. If successful, Commission members feel these efforts can increase understanding of the importance of local planning and lend it greater local support.

Recently, the Commission embarked on two public education and information programs to achieve these goals, supported by substantial federal funding. The Commission has also undertaken other education and information activities. The Commission's past public forums were in some respects promotional, but they also provided Tug Hill citizens with direct access to the Commission. In addition, the Commission publishes an occasional newsletter, offers press releases, speaks to interested groups on regional issues, and generates other publicity on regional issues and Commission activities.

One project, funded by the National Science Foundation's (NSF) Science for Citizens program, was designed to provide citizens in two cooperative planning board areas with science information on public issues by use of slide shows, map displays, field trips, and public workshops.[20] In addition, the U.S. Department of Health, Education, and Welfare (HEW) Office of Education funded educational workshops so that planning boards in these same two cooperative areas could convey information to the public.[21]

The total of these two federal grants for a year and a half is nearly $45,000, enough to hire a full-time education coordinator to manage the projects. The Commission hoped these two programs would help rural residents make effective use of environmental information and help tailor this information to the needs of rural people. In practice, the two grants have built on each other.[22]

The Salmon Rivers (SRCPB) and Jefferson County Snowbelt (JCSB) cooperative planning boards established steering committees in the spring of 1979, comprised of board members and other interested citizens, such as teachers and a county forester. These committees planned and executed the programs with Commission assistance, making specific decisions regarding what would most likely appeal to residents in their communities. The steering committees also reviewed all materials prepared by the Commission and by the nearby State University Research Corporation (SURCO) at SUNY Oswego.

The SRCPB selected water quality as its community workshop topic. It directed numerous other activities as well. A separate workshop on "using local environmental planning to make the classroom come alive" was attended by ten teachers. Under the HEW grant, SURCO prepared seven easy-to-read booklets on issues in local water quality, which were widely distributed.[23] A traveling poster and map display illustrating the area's land use, topography, hydrology, and history rotated throughout the summer to town fairs, public meetings, and local businesses. Slide tape shows on local natural resources and the planning process were also prepared; their outlines were developed by the steering committee. And 100 cars followed a drive-it-yourself tour of the six municipalities, arranged for an early September Saturday.

The JCSB focused its workshop on the trade-off between local agriculture and residential development, putting together a panel of four speakers, presenting both sides of the issue. It conducted many of the same activities as SRCPB. To emphasize educating the area's youth, two high school assembly programs were held. The JCSB also prepared a traveling map display and a slide tape show on local resources. In addition, the JCSB arranged for five local newspaper essays and fifteen radio spots in local media on issues to be raised in the late April workshops. These were previewed by twenty-one local officials and served both as public information and advertisement for the workshop. And a drive-it-yourself tour included local parks, firehalls, a cheese factory, sawmill, and dairy farm. School programs and "public inquiry" meetings involving students and adults are planned for the last six months of the pilot program. An outside evaluation of the total program is a part of the NSF grant.

The need for these extensive education programs was apparently identified by Commission staff. One cooperative board member commented on the program's origin, "The Commission did it, but we knew we needed it." One of the cooperative boards was about to present its draft comprehensive plan for public review. And in at least one town, public misunderstanding of a proposed zoning ordinance had seriously hurt the planning board's morale and its reputation with the town board. The Commission apparently reasoned that the participation and support of a town's citizens is eventually needed to enact any local land use regulation. Further, the momentum of a concrete project could provide motivation and focus for a cooperative board.

How successful were these programs? The two SRCPB water quality workshops, held in March and early April, attracted only about twenty-five citizens, other than those involved in their planning. The JCSB workshop fared somewhat better, with about forty attending, including all three town supervisors. The drive-it-yourself tours and teachers' workshops were well received. It is difficult to estimate the impact of the map displays, brochures, slide tape shows, and news essays and radio spots on Tug Hill citizens. While turnout was low, those attending these events were highly satisfied.

COMMUNITY ORGANIZING AND COMMUNICATION

The Commission provides cooperative planning boards and their member local planning boards not just with planning services, but also with assistance in organizing their board and communicating among themselves, with their town boards, and with the community.

This help is provided through the field staff and backed by the technical assistance program previously described.

This aspect of the Commission's local planning and development programs may be more important to building long-term local capabilities than technical planning assistance. The Commission's role in community organizing and communication in these rural towns has, in the minds of Commission staff, grown increasingly important to the program's overall effectiveness. Rural towns, especially those with no prior planning experience, cannot concentrate on planning without first organizing properly for the task and communicating with their town board. Further, the very existence of cooperative planning boards can foster increased communication between towns.

Commission involvement in community organizing began with formation of the first cooperative board. None of the nine towns interested had ever formed a local planning board or gone through the legal, organizational, administrative, and procedural tasks necessary to operate such a joint effort. To even translate the desire for joint action into the reality of a joint planning board required a massive organizational effort by the Commission staff. And throughout the complex planning process, professional help was necessary to assist with procedures, supply legal information, help with the mechanics of the planning process, and help boost flagging motivations. This substantial assistance was provided partly through Commission planning and community assistance staff, and partly through a circuit rider, previously described.[24] As one staff member put it, "If there was a crisis in a town, we practically lived, night and day, in that town until the problem was solved."

This type of aid appeared to be so integral to the CTHPB's planning process that the Commission now strives to arrange for a full-time rural aide/coordinator for each cooperative board in addition to a planner. Presently, three of the five cooperative boards are staffed by rural aides, though all three are relatively new to their jobs. The principle is simple: by maintaining a person the planning boards can trust in the town, a variety of needs can be met. This presence often begins before a cooperative board's formation and may well need to continue as long as the cooperative board is functioning.

By maintaining contact with as many planning boards, town boards, and town residents as possible, the Commission hopes to

Rural aide confers with Orwell town supervisor.

develop improved links within and between towns, immediate and long-term support for cooperative planning, a higher level of planning board motivation, and informal influence for broader land use decisions. One Commission staff member described an important aspect of the job as "getting town boards and planning boards together." This involves spending much time in people's kitchens. For example, the first assignment for one new rural aide was door to door visits to many town residents, being referred by one to the next, to talk about the town, its future, and present problems and issues. Besides introducing the new rural aide, this process was aimed at opening communications and reducing suspicion of a newcomer.

Another major task is guiding planning boards through complex unfamiliar procedures. For example, a major effort was undertaken in the fall of 1979 to assist cooperative boards in submitting their funding requests effectively and on time so that they would be included in town budgets. Likewise, much effort was spent visiting town boards with local planning board members to explain and build support for official signing of intermunicipal agreements (IMA) that allow the cooperative boards to legally function.[25] Commission staff feel that the procedural aspects of local planning can hinder local governments' efforts if no aid is provided.

A third major organizational service of the rural aide and Commission staff involves paperwork and the mechanics of operating a planning board. One cooperative planning board member remarked, "I just don't have time for all that paperwork." Someone has to write agendas, review minutes, schedule meetings and hearings, and keep contact with members over long distances. In populous suburban towns outside Tug Hill, these activities are often handled by a full-time town clerk and secretary.

A fourth aspect of the Commission's efforts to aid planning board communication is the emphasis on conducting opinion surveys of local residents on topics related to the land use planning program. These citizen surveys are aimed at gaining insight into the feeling of residents on major town issues and what actions they are willing to take on them. Surveys, if conducted properly, can provide valuable back up for a planning board in convincing is town board of the wisdom of its recommendations. They can guide cooperative boards in resolving issues of mutual concern, and seek out prevailing opinion beyond that of vocal minorities.[26]

The need for all these types of organizational and communications assistance, in at least some Tug Hill communities, is apparent. Frequently, those involved in Commission planning programs stress the importance of this aid in allowing them to concentrate on planning decisions. And those groups that have completed citizen surveys find them a useful tool. Nonetheless, efforts to foster communication among the cooperative boards, member planning boards, and their local governing boards have not been completely successful in the case of every cooperative board, as discussed in Chapter 4.

ADDRESSING BROADER ISSUES

Study of the entire Tug Hill region was emphasized in the Tug Hill Commission's 1972 mandate. This has been addressed by identifying, publicizing, studying, and recommending actions on particular issues potentially significant to much of the Tug Hill study region—rather than by developing a formal, regional plan. Through this activity, the Commission hopes to provide a broader perspective on Tug Hill land use issues.

But the amount of time, money, and effort commissioners and staff devote to this task has varied over the years. Early on, the Commission heavily emphasized regional policy research, as it developed its 1976 recommendations to the state legislature and the governor. After a period when regionwide issues received little attention, this area of activity is growing again in prominence.

The Commission currently serves several functions in this area. For one, it identifies and keeps up to date on state-level issues potentially important to local governments and citizens of the Tug Hill area. It often transmits this information in some manner to local governments within the region. The Commission also acts as a spokesman for Tug Hill to the state. As such, Commission staff attend state legislative committee hearings on appropriate topics and prepare testimony on many issues.

In addition, the Commission occasionally organizes conferences around regional issues, such as its cosponsorship of a September 1978 conference on the future of Oneida Lake.[27] And it sometimes seeks grant money to work on issues it sees as regionally important, such as a recent effort to obtain federal Department of Energy funding to investigate wind power generation on Tug Hill.[28]

Recently, the Commission has begun research on several issues it considers to be of regional importance. For example, a major study on the real property tax system will include updated land market data, estimation of tax shifts in Tug Hill lands due to upcoming full value reassessment, alternative taxing policies for forest and agricultural lands, and the possible relationship between the cost of public services and taxes for different classes of property. Another current effort, in the area of economic development, assesses the economic feasibility of moose ranching as a commercial venture.[29]

In the past, the Commission has examined a number of diverse issues, from the social and economic impacts of 765 kv transmission lines to acid precipitation and its effects in the Tug Hill area. Often consultants have provided expertise for all or part of the research on specific issues.

The Commission is also considering possible future arrangements for continuing its present programs after its scheduled phase-

Photograph courtesy of W. H. Kennedy, Jr.

out date. In September 1977, the Commission decided to complete its work and phase out its operations by March 31, 1981.[30] By that time the commissioners felt that every town would have had opportunity to join a cooperative planning board. Independence from the Commission was felt to be an important goal, and long-term support programs might not require a continuing regional commission.

As part of Commission efforts to develop recommendations to the state legislature for the long-term future of its programs, two workshops were held in November 1979 to hear the views of 125 local residents and officials about the future of the Commission's programs.[31] Two subregional committees on transition policy, comprised of local community leaders, were then formed to review alternatives for the long-term future of the Commission's programs. The Commission is also developing alternatives to transfer some programs to existing local agencies. As with its 1976 recommendations, the emphasis is on local involvement.

THE COMMISSION'S OPERATION

The evolution and operation of the Commission's program have been significantly influenced by the nature of Commission membership and staffing, funding sources and strategies, and characteristics of the Commission's political support base.

COMMISSION MEMBERSHIP

The attitudes of the initial Commission members were a major factor in setting direction in both approach and programs. The Tug Hill Commission has followed this direction to this day. Individual commissioners are still a force in setting the overall policy and tone of its activities.

The original Commission was made up entirely of residents of the Commission's study area. The only exception was the late assembly member Crawford who resided nearby in Oswego. Only one member was not a long-term or lifetime resident of a Tug Hill county. The commissioners represented a variety of informal interest groups in the Tug Hill area. Many held influential positions in county politics or business. All owned some property in the Tug Hill area. In addition, all possessed local or state-level political connections.[32]

How was such a locally oriented state commission appointed? The first list of possible Commission members was drawn by Crawford, an influential Republican central to the Commission's formation. He passed it on to the three state officials responsible for Commission appointments: the governor, senate temporary president, and assembly Speaker. It appears that no changes were made in Crawford's carefully balanced list (see Table 3.3).

The first commissioners represented all four Tug Hill counties proportionately by population, land area, and major area interest groups. In addition, three of the appointees had been involved in the Commission's formation (see Table 3.4).

Overall, the Commission membership list satisfied most of those who cared at that time. A few complaints noted that the Commission was perhaps dominated by commercial interests and that farmers, loggers, and residents from the core area of Tug Hill were not adequately represented.[33]

TABLE 3.3

Tug Hill Commission Members
(listed in order of their appointment to the Commission)

Name	Office Held	Appointed By	Dates of Service
Carle, George E.[a]	Chairman 1975–77	Governor	to May 1977
Colvin, John F.[a]		Governor	to May 1977
Cox, Sidney T.[a]	Vice-Chairman 1975–79 (Acting Chairman 1977–78)	Assembly	to August 1979
Crawford, Edward F.[a]	Chairman 1973–75	Assembly	to Sept. 1975
Goetz, Joseph A.[a]		Assembly	to August 1978
Karcher, Urban N.[a]		Senate	all
Lansing, Livingston[a]		Senate	all
Mark, Richard E.[a]	Chairman 1978–present	Senate	all
Smith, A. Milain[a]		Governor	to May 1977
McMahon, James M.		Assembly	from May 1976
Greene, Blanche M.		Governor	from May 1977
Maloney, Bernard E.		Governor	from May 1977
Rich, Stephen L.	Secretary 1978–present	Governor	from May 1977
Taylor, William J.		Assembly	from August 1978
Bowman, Jane T.		Assembly	from August 1979

[a]Original members

Sources: Temporary State Commission on Tug Hill, *Interim Report* (Watertown, N.Y.: March 1974), and *Preparing for the Future* (Watertown, N.Y.: February 1976); Watertown *Daily Times*, March 21, 1973, and June 27, 1978; Syracuse *Post Standard*, May 15, 1977.

Early on, a few major attitudes of most commissioners about their role, purpose, and the Tug Hill area under study emerged. At the first few Commission meetings, besides a strong desire to protect Tug Hill from exploitation, the commissioners voiced an equally strong commitment to "providing ample, frequent opportunities for citizen input into the ideas and deliberations of the Commission"[34] and to the importance and the need for cooperation and communica-

TABLE 3.4

Residences and Occupations of Tug Hill Commission Members
(listed in order of their appointment to the Commission)

Name	Municipality and County of Residence	Occupation	Party
Carle, George E. [a]	Camden-Oneida	Concrete manufacturing firm owner, town councilman	R
Colvin, John F. [a]	Copenhagen-Lewis	Former turbine operator, paper co.; county legislator	R
Cox, Sidney T. [a]	Turin-Lewis	Former State Assembly Ways & Means Committee staff, composer	R
Crawford, Edward F. [a]	Oswego-Oswego	State assemblyman; attorney	R
Goetz, Joseph A. [a]	Lee-Oneida	Sales representative; Town Board member	D
Karcher, Urban N. [a]	Castorland-Lewis	County treasurer and budget officer; village clerk	R
Lansing, Livingston [a]	Boonville-Oneida	Newspaper and radio station owner; motel owner; weather specialist; former Adirondack Study Commissioner	R
Mark, Richard E. [a]	Constantia-Oswego	College professor (forestry)	R
Smith, A. Milian [a]	Watertown-Jefferson	Real estate; former turkey farmer	R
McMahon, James M.	Hastings-Oswego	Dairy farmer; former town supervisor	D
Greene, Blanche M.	Rodman-Jefferson	Postmaster (retired); former Democratic Committee member	D
Maloney, Bernard E.	Florence-Oneida	Welder and steamfitter; former county and town supervisor; Democratic Committeeman	D
Rich, Stephen L.	Watertown-Jefferson	Banker, town councilman	D
Taylor, William J.	Lee-Oneida	Business treasurer and director (retired); former town supervisor and planning board chairman, former county comptroller	D
Bowman, Jane T.	West Carthage-Jefferson	Business accounting manager, Democratic Committee member	D

[a]Original members

Sources: Temporary State Commission on Tug Hill, *Interim Report* (Watertown, N.Y.: March 1976), and *Preparing for the Future* (Watertown, N.Y.: February 1976); Watertown *Daily Times*, March 21, 1973, and June 7, 1978.

tion with local officials. They were receptive to local interests and concerns, as previously noted. While the commissioners apparently had few preconceptions as to possible recommendations, they did exhibit a basic commitment to the role of local government in land use decision-making. One commissioner phrased it, "We were conscious of the kind of rural people we had to deal with."

Most commissioners have been active and sincere participants in the group's decisions. While many decisions have been far from unanimous, the Commission has taken a forceful role in setting policy, and exhibits strong commitment as a group and as individuals to its charge and objectives. Several commissioners were firm about their role in making decisions for staff to then carry out. In one commissioner's words, appointees are "not political hacks."

The present Commission has six new replacements for original members. In the course of eight years, its leadership has also changed. In 1977 the three governor-appointed members were replaced by Democratic Governor Carey. A year earlier an active farmer was appointed to replace assembly member Crawford after his death. In 1978, and again in 1979, the assembly Speaker replaced original members. The new members primarily add representation from the core area, farming, and local government.

Three people have chaired the Commission. Crawford was the first chairman. The present chairman, Richard Mark, was elected in 1978. This follows three years during which George A. Carle, a Camden construction firm owner and the first vice-chairman, served as chairman.[35] For the most part, the Commission still functions in the same manner and with the same goals as did the original group.

What types of people were appointed to this regional commission? What motivated them to serve? As a partial answer, profiles of four past and present commissioners follow. Two, Richard Mark and George Carle, have chaired the Commission. The other two, Livingston Lansing and Urban Karcher, have been on the Commission since its formation and offer somewhat different perspectives on its purpose.

Richard Mark was actively involved in the Commission's creation. A SUNY professor of forestry, he is oriented to the natural resource aspects of the Commission's charge and to planning as one part of a regional program. He has lived in the Tug Hill area in the town of Constantia, Oswego County, since 1970. He sees an innova-

Photograph courtesy of David M. Doody.

tive Commission, representing not just statewide interests, but one exploring regional issues in a unique area. "This area is just different enough to deserve special attention."

George Carle, born in Altmar, became involved partly because he knew Crawford through the local political system and partly out of concern for state intervention. He sees the Commission's role as to "keep things the way they are, to protect the people living here. You can't stop growth, but plan for it. We should keep Tug Hill a place where people want to stay."

Urban Karcher, a lifetime Tug Hill area resident, has often been called "Mr. Lewis County," in recognition of his long and active involvement in local and county politics. Presently Lewis County treasurer and budget officer, he has held a variety of local and county elected positions. He is a strong voice on the Commission, speaking for coordination with local governments and assistance with their needs. He is a practical man with a strong political sense.

Liv Lansing was born in Minnesota, but his family originally settled in the Tug Hill area. Educated outside this area, he is involved in many local projects. He is owner and operator of radio station WBRV, a local newspaper, and the new Boonville motel, and is a former Chamber of Commerce president. He is a U.S. Weather Service cooperative observer and has been a snow surveyor for more than twenty-five years. His concern for the region's economic health and natural resource base, as well as experience on the Adirondack Study Commission, led him to support the Commission's formation and volunteer to serve on it. A forward-thinking individual, he sees the Commission as a varied group, and his own views less "preservationist" than some, but feels the mix of interests represented is a good one. While he is very positive about the Commission's achievements, he is willing to hear diverse views.

STAFFING

The staff assembled by the Tug Hill Commission to carry out its locally oriented programs is a highly visible component of the Commission's day-to-day operations. Often the staff is a local government's first contact with the Commission, and they can shape reactions to the agency. The Commission chose a service-oriented staff, beginning with the executive director. This attitude of service extends both to Tug Hill local governments and to the Commission itself.[36]

The Commission staff, in general, has been selected both for technical competence in a particular field and also for attitude. As a result, by all accounts, virtually all past and present staff members have displayed a strong commitment to the Commission's work, and a dedication to working with local governments and region residents. Although the staff spans a variety of disciplines, with very few exceptions, staff attitude and performance have been viewed favorably by those in contact with them.

The commissioners apparently used the hiring of the executive director to, in the words of one commissioner, "sort out our priorities and orientation." They considered a range of applicants, from planners to career state employees. The director they hired was not trained as a planner. Instead, Benjamin Coe was vice-president of a private nonprofit social and economic development group, Volunteers in Technical Assistance (VITA), with a self-help approach. He was thus familiar with community type programs and local government work.

The Commission next hired a community participation coordinator and a natural resource planner, both with equal responsibility to direct programs. The former was an area native formerly with the New York State Farm Bureau; the latter was a professional planner with a nearby county planning department.[37] In addition, Cooperative Extension helped fund a coordinator to work for the CTHPB.

From this modest beginning, Commission staff has grown as programs have expanded. The staff in June 1979 consisted of five planners, six community participation staff, a technical assistance coordinator, a coordinator for the citizen education project, two cartographers, two natural resource policy analysts, and support staff (see Figure 3.1). The staff is least strong in the economic development field.

Some staff members are long-term local residents; all are professionally trained in some field. Most commonly, each cooperative planning board is served by a team made up of at least one planner and one community participation staff member. Thus the commission staff is organized by function as indicated in the organization chart, Figure 3.1, but with geographically oriented teams cutting across functional lines.

By March 1980, the Commission had established shared staff arrangements with three planning agencies: the Oneida and Oswego County planning departments and the Black River-St. Lawrence Regional Planning Board.[38] The arrangements improve communication with these agencies and may provide a base for continuing planning assistance after 1981. Six of the Commission's staff members, including three of the rural aides, are CETA-funded through county Manpower programs.

Only once was a Commission staff member inappropriate for the job. While technically competent, the person's manner of dealing with planning board members did not reflect the Commission's hard-earned image of local service and offended some local board members. One long-term cooperative planning board member com-

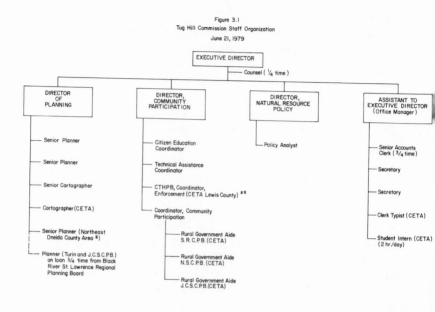

Figure 3.1
Tug Hill Commission Staff Organization
June 21, 1979

* Stationed at Oneida County Planning Office
** Stationed at Lewis County Highway Department

mented, "If they were all like that, I would not have stayed on the planning board." This staff member was eventually replaced.

More common staff attitudes on planning and on how to work with people are illustrated by one staff member's comment: "We don't play almighty expert; we show them the alternatives. We let them make the decisions and decide what to do on their own." One staff planner described this as a "humanistic approach to planning and assistance; we try to deal with individuals."

FUNDING: Sources and Uses

The Commission received the majority of its program money directly from the State of New York, through annual appropriations to the Commission in the state's executive or supplemental budget. This has totaled $1.35 million for the six years 1974–80 (see Table

3.5). In addition, the Commission has attracted $111,000 in grants and another $171,000 for CETA employees.[39]

State funding has increased over the course of the Commission's survival, as its program has expanded. State money comes without any formal strings, except for program goals the Commission outlines for itself in its annual budget request, and excluding the implicit threat of a cut off in state funds if state objectives are violated. State appropriations have grown from $50,000 in 1973, to $350,000 in 1979.

The Commission does not rely heavily on the federal regional program money that sustains many regional agencies, such as funding for HUD 701 comprehensive planning, criminal justice planning, or any of nearly forty other programs. Nor has it deliberately focused on obtaining grants for Tug Hill communities or on aggressively pursuing grants for its own support or for specific projects.

However, the Commission has still managed to expand its total

TABLE 3.5

Annual State Appropriations to the Tug Hill Commission

Fiscal Year	Amount Appropriated	Date Approved	Form of Appropriation	Amount Requested
1972–73	$ 5,000	May 22	Supplemental Budget	
1973–74	$ 50,000	June 23, 1973	Supplemental Budget	$100,000
	$ 5,000	February 1974	Deficiency Budget	
1974–75	$125,000	March 26	Executive Budget	$234,000
	$ 50,000	June 15	Supplemental Budget	
1975–76	$175,000	March	Executive Budget	$351,526
1976–77	$175,000	March 16	Executive Budget	$175,000
1977–78	$175,000	March	Executive Budget	$246,000
	$ 50,000	July 27	Supplemental Budget	
1978–79	$250,000	March	Executive Budget	$250,000
1979–80	$350,000	April 5	Executive Budget	$342,000
1980–81	$365,000	March	Executive Budget	$365,000

Source: New York State annual budgets and Tug Hill Commission funding requests.

available funds by more than 7 percent over its eight-year history, through obtaining several major grants, primarily from federal agencies channeled through the state. More than a quarter of this grant money has been transferred to other institutions, often local, such as the State University at Oswego and Oneida County Cooperative Extension. The six major grants received are listed in Table 3.6.

Another 10 percent increase in the Commission's funds comes through extensive use of CETA funds to hire local unemployed residents. Much of this money has been used for rural aides. In addition, towns in several of the cooperative planning areas make annual contributions to their cooperative board budgets.

TABLE 3.6

Grants Received by the Tug Hill Commission

Source	Amount	Purpose	Dates
U.S. Dept. of Housing and Urban Development (via N.Y.S. Office of Planning Services)	$ 15,000	Citizen participation, public forums	1973–75
U.S. Dept. of Housing and Urban Development (via N.Y.S. Dept. of State)	$ 8,717	Property tax study, land use policy study	1976–77
Federal Intergovernmental Personnel Act (via N.Y.S. Dept. of State)	$ 18,211	Circuit rider technical assistance program	1977–79
Federal Intergovernmental Personnel Act (via N.Y.S. Sept. of State)	$ 35,637	Pilot county technical assistance program	1979–80
U.S. Dept. of Health, Education, and Welfare, Environmental Education	$ 18,437	Citizen education	1978–80
National Science Foundation, Science for Citizens Program	$ 29,954	Citizen education	1978–80
	$125,956		

Source: Tug Hill Commission.

The Commission also assists cooperative planning boards and local communities to attract grant money of their own, much of it previously inaccessible. Nearly $10,000 of foundation and Cooperative Extension money went into the CTHPB's early years.[40] Through Commission assistance, the town of Rodman built a new water supply system with a $233,000 federal Economic Development Administration grant. While the size of this particular grant is unusual, the Commission has aided at least twenty-one communities in preparing successful grant proposals for local projects.

How has the Commission used its money? One major expenditure is staff time, particularly for the cooperative planning program and supplemental services such as technical assistance.

Development of regional policy, at first the only Commission use of professional staff time, dropped to a low of 6 percent of the total salaries spent in 1976, but has now risen to 14 percent. Planning and technical assistance, in contrast, has averaged nearly 50 percent of the staff program time since 1974, with other community work adding another 35 percent.[41] So, although the Commission has not made direct grants to individual towns or to cooperative groups, it has heavily subsidized local planning programs, particularly in cooperative planning board areas. This has been its single biggest expenditure of state money. Much of the rest has gone to administrative overhead, and to consultants for specialized research, often on regionwide issues.

Attempts to assess the return to local communities from Tug Hill Commission dollars are not productive. Clearly, the smaller towns in the core area with lowest population and least capability to purchase these services have gained the most directly. But the worth of this improved local capability to other towns in the Tug Hill area, that have received less direct assistance, is hard to measure. Comparisons with budgets of other regional commissions created for similar purposes are also not fruitful, for the Tug Hill Commission program is different.

POLITICAL SURVIVAL

The Tug Hill Commission has survived for eight years without the major political conflict that has characterized other similar recent temporary regional commissions in New York State. It has been annually extended by the state legislature. Despite occasional budget crises, it has received funding each year. And a formal legislative extension has not been required since 1974.

In contrast to the Commission's creation, its continuation results from support of a variety of groups within the region, especially those directly served by its programs, that has grown since the Commission's early years. This local support has been expressed at the state level through strong and active Commission support by influential legislators from the region, at first by former assembly member Crawford and more recently by Senator Barclay. At the same time, active opposition to the Commission's activities from within or outside the region has not been heard at the state level. Without the Commission's strategy of broad local support and a low state-level profile, its survival might be in question.

Temporary state commissions in New York are typically extended either by specific legislation granting authority to a certain date, or through appropriations in the legislature's supplementary budget. Seeking funding through legislative additions to the executive budget is the least controversial but most unpredictable route. It requires strong political support with the legislature, a lack of conflict regarding the program, and a strong program that is presented effectively to budget officials. The Commission has succeeded in this strategy each year since 1974.

One senator from the region, Senator Barclay, exerts his considerable influence on behalf of the Commission. Other region legislators support the Commission's budget request with colleagues, but those interviewed stressed Barclay's key role.

Thus the Commission has not required a formal legislative extension through separate legislation since 1974. By avoiding the introduction of specific enabling legislation, the Commission can sidestep the question of adequate statewide support. The major effort involved in organizing passage of special legislation, requiring individual decisions by each state legislator as to the Commission's merits, is also avoided.

One of the most difficult periods for the Commission's obtaining state funds was early 1975, at the time it was developing its preliminary recommendations. The Commission was reinstated in the 1975–76 executive budget by legislative action, although at half the amount originally requested.

The new Democratic governor, Hugh Carey, did not include the Tug Hill Commission, along with several other temporary state commissions, in his 1975 executive budget. This did not indicate his opposition to this particular commission, but rather a desire to distinguish his administration from the previous one and a feeling that legislatively created commissions should be legislatively maintained.

In addition, the state assembly had a new Democratic majority, and the number of Democratic senators had increased. The atmosphere in Albany was not conducive to the survival of Republican-formed temporary commissions. Budgeting was extremely tight, and programs with little apparent support were most affected.

The Commission, to show that its work was in need of state funding, turned to the region for bipartisan support from the people it served. It received supporting resolutions or letters from many groups, among them: all four county legislatures or boards of supervisors; seven of the eight Democratic and Republican party chairmen; the Cooperative Tug Hill Planning Board; a group of eight town supervisors from the region, balanced by political party and county representation; several individual town boards and planning boards; and at least one county planning department.[42] Most daily and weekly newspapers serving this area provided editorial support. In addition, the commissioner of DEC lobbied behind the scenes for the group's continuation. And previous Commission grants from the Department of State and Office of Planning Services likely influenced the budget process, although these agencies did not actively support the Commission at this time.

Senator Barclay forcefully and skillfully exerted influence on the Commission's behalf. In addition to lobbying for funds, he and another area senator, James Donovan, pushed a bill through the senate to extend the Commission in the event money was not appropriated in the executive budget.[43] Senator Barclay's strong support of the Commission, backed by evidence of strong local support and no local opposition, resulted in the Commission's presence in the 1975 executive budget. This example illustrates how support within the region has contributed to the Commission's political survival at the state level.

4 The Commission's Impact: Cooperative Planning In Five Areas

THE TUG HILL COMMISSION has channeled most of its programs through the activities of five cooperative planning boards, whose formation the Commission actively fostered. As of January 1980, these boards involved twenty-six area towns and five villages (see Table 4.1 and Map 10). Towns and villages are encouraged, through the Commission's assistance pι grams, to join formally together to prepare joint plans and discuss issues of common interest. The Commission provides these boards with technical, planning, organizational, and educational assistance with no formal strings, often at minimum cost to the member towns. But there is presently no one "model" of how planning is conducted with these boards.

Cooperative planning began with nine towns in the core area of Tug Hill. The first cooperative board was in part a local idea, and highly experimental. It was not, in the words of one commissioner, "something we sat down and did research on."

Rather, at the suggestion of one town supervisor, officials from ten core towns met in June 1974 to consider a joint planning effort to protect their resources and to retain local decision-making without state control. By that October, nine towns in four different counties formed individual town planning boards and elected representatives to a Cooperative Tug Hill Planning Board.[1] The CTHPB was organized and financed largely by the Tug Hill Commission and provided with technical support.

The Commission seized on this effort as a possible way to develop a formal regional plan and land use regulations emphasizing the natural resource base. It proposed to divide the rest of the thirty-

TABLE 4.1

Cooperative Planning Boards in the Tug Hill Region

Name of Planning Board	Towns and Villages	Counties Involved	Date Formed	1970 Population	Current Program Activities (Dec. 1979)
Cooperative Tug Hill	Boylston[a] Florence Montague Osceola Pinckney Redfield[a] West Turin Worth Lewis[c] Turin/Turin Village[c,d]	Jefferson Lewis Oneida Oswego	Oct. 1974 〉 Nov. 1978	5,319 1,454	administering rural development code community inventories
Salmon Rivers Cooperative	Albion/Altmar Village[d] Orwell Parish/Parish Village[d] Williamstown[b]	Oswego	May 1976	4,953	formulating ordinances, citizen education
North Shore Cooperative	Central Square Village Cleveland Village Constantia[b] Hastings Vienna West Monroe	Oneida Oswego	May 1977	16,103	community inventories, individual regulations
Jefferson County Snowbelt Cooperative	Adams Lorraine Rodman	Jefferson	Nov. 1977	5,781	community inventories, citizen education
Northeast Oneida	Floyd Lee Steuben Western	Oneida	Aug. 1978	12,522	revising old ordinances
Total Population				46,132	

[a]These towns have not adopted the Rural Development Code.
[b]These towns joined their cooperative planning board afater it was formed.
[c]New members accepted into CTHPB July 1979.
[d]Joint town/village planning board.

Sources: Tug Hill Commission and 1970 U.S. Census data. Information as of December 1979.

nine-town area into groups of towns with common interests and require each group to produce a plan by a certain date. In this way the pieces could be put together to produce the areawide plan. However, Commission members and staff gradually realized that this idea would be unworkable for Tug Hill. The CTHPB's success did prompt the Commission to stimulate the formation of four other

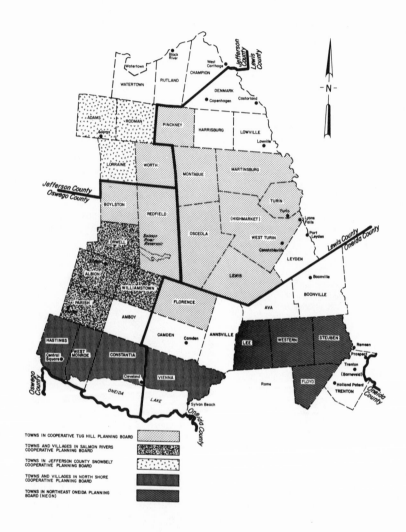

TABLE 4.2

1970 Population in Tug Hill Counties

County	Population in Cooperative Planning Board Areas	Population outside Cooperative Planning Board Areas	Tug Hill Area Total
Jefferson	5,966	9,845	15,811
Lewis	5,316	9,221	14,537
Oneida	17,111	15,776	32,887
Oswego	17,739	557	18,296
Total	46,132	35,399	81,531

subregional groups of towns. At this time thirteen towns and fifteen villages in the Tug Hill are not involved in any cooperative planning program (see Table 4.2).

Once viewed by the Commission as a potential "model" for others, the CTHPB experience has not transferred directly to other cooperative boards, however. Many variations exist among the boards in purpose and activities, as well as in the areas they serve. While the CTHPB's main activity was to prepare a comprehensive rural development code, which has been adopted by seven of its member towns, other cooperative boards have a completely different approach to working together.

Commission staff now state, from experience, that flexibility is important in working with these cooperative boards. "Not all cooperative boards and their towns need a comprehensive plan and ordinances. The point is to help them learn how to deal with their problems, how to determine when they need help, and where to find it."[2] Planning is thus conducted on a voluntary basis with no specific products required and no time deadlines.

The character of the communities involved, attitudes of their residents, and degree of identification with their neighboring communities are important considerations. Many local variations exist among the five groups of communities in past planning experience, social and economic characteristics, and the nature of their physical resource base. Each cooperative board's set of goals differs as does

In the Tug Hill upland, pressures come from seasonal camp and second home development. *Photograph courtesy of W. H. Kennedy, Jr.*

motivation, task, function, results, and even the name chosen to identify itself. Furthermore, links between the cooperative board, local planning boards, and town governing boards also vary greatly.

COOPERATIVE TUG HILL PLANNING BOARD:
Protecting the Core Area

Nine towns in four different counties formed the first cooperative planning board in 1974. Since then, two additional towns have asked to join.[3] This group's experience formed the basis for Commission interest in trying a cooperative planning process throughout the Tug Hill area. The CTHPB's experience is documented in the case study, "Cooperative Rural Planning," by Elizabeth Marsh. At least a portion of each of these nine towns is in the traditional Tug Hill core area, which differs substantially from the rest of the study region.

These are the most rural, sparsely populated, and isolated towns:

A 1976 meeting of Cooperative Tug Hill Planning Board held at the Pinckney Town Hall. *Photograph courtesy of W. H. Kennedy, Jr.*

nearly three-quarters forested, with some abandoned agricultural land and much state-owned forest. The number of seasonal camps almost equals the number of permanent homes. In Montague, Redfield, and Worth, two-thirds of the private landowners are nonresidents. Five landowners own half the private land in Redfield.[4]

Permanent inhabitants tend to be long-term, if not lifetime, residents. More than half of those with jobs commute out of the nine towns. At the 1974 public forums, these people were among the most vocal in their desire for no change and for local control.

Massive economic or population growth is not seen as likely here. With low tax incomes, local governments are usually limited to providing a few basic services, mainly road maintenance. These towns had no prior experience with planning or with land use controls, and none had a formal planning board.

Why did these towns form the CTHPB? Each town board had individual reasons for agreeing to the cooperative venture. But most saw the board's formation as a move to protect their town resources, their life styles, and their authority. Importantly, the people who were instrumental in forming this cooperative board were also town board members. Town boards saw at least two outside threats to their towns: development, including new residents and camp owners; and the threat of state intervention, including the Tug Hill Commission itself.

A CTHPB representative and former town board member, whose town at first strongly resisted the cooperative board, said, "The town board felt they had to do this, that there was no choice with the state coming in." A former CTHPB chairman described its purpose as "to do something before the state does it for us." At least one original CTHPB member was there to work against zoning; one Commission staff member noted that planning and land use regulation were "initially the furthest thing from any of their minds." The then Redfield town supervisor and county legislator, often credited with the idea for the cooperative board, appeared to some to be interested mostly in getting assistance and keeping the state out. A Rome *Sentinel* headline summed it up: "Tug Hill towns plan their future before State does it for them."[5]

Besides the threats of development and state intervention, the towns had other concerns. Some of these can be inferred from goals of the CTHPB's resource management plan, their main policy statement. The overall goal of "Keep Tug Hill Like It Is" was to be carried out by maintaining forest resources, protecting wetlands and streams, maintaining active agriculture, and restricting new development to hamlets and along existing roads.[6]

What else did the nine towns hope to gain from a cooperative planning board? Their plan identifies several benefits: preserving home rule; considering land uses that cross town boundaries; increasing influence by banding together; reducing the cost of planning; and increasing the likelihood of enforcement against pressures of interest groups.[7]

The Commission supported the CTHPB technically, organizationally, and financially. Uncertainty and bargaining on both sides was involved as the cooperative board took shape. Each town contributed $400, as recommended by Commission staff, toward a tentative six-month operating budget of $15,000. The rest was supplied by the Commission outright or through tapping other funding sources for this experimental effort.[8] This included funding for a coordinator whose activities were directed by the CTHPB.

Though the CTHPB at first relied heavily on professional guid-

The Tug Hill forest stretches unbroken by roads in an area close to twenty miles on a side. Dark patches are the evergreens. *Photograph courtesy of David M. Doody.*

ance, the Commission staff emphasized members' involvement, confidence, and eventual independence. The CTHPB thus drove through their towns, conducting "windshield" surveys of existing land uses and opinion surveys of their neighbors. They wrote and revised, word for word, the entire resource management plan and rural development code. All information and drafts were reviewed at both the cooperative and town levels. This direct involvement of board members in learning how to collect information and turn it into a plan, rather than simply reacting to professionals' work, increased members' self-reliance. How difficult and time consuming was this? "Try drafting something with eighteen people," replied one Commission staff member. The entire planning process took three and a half years.

The CTHPB officially declared its independence of the Tug Hill Commission in November 1976, through a formal resolution. After the plan was drafted and while implementation was being discussed, old suspicions of the Commission and the state re-emerged in some towns. This, combined with higher confidence of planning board members in their new roles, led to desire for a more formal relationship with the Commission. Thereafter, all Commission assistance was by request only.

The CTHPB's 1976 plan was based directly on land capabilities and a natural resource inventory of the shared forests and watersheds. Discussion of ways to implement the plan came well before the plan was approved. Many alternatives were considered, and suspicion of joint land use controls was strong. A former CTHPB chairman put it this way: "The idea of working together to plan for the future wasn't fully trusted or understood. . . . We weren't sure we needed controls."[9] But, as the plan states, "The CTHPB has selected the field of land use controls as the initial way in which to implement the Plan."[10]

The joint controls agreed upon were written up as a comprehensive model rural development code. This code contains strong environmental protection regulations, such as timber harvesting restrictions, regulations for activities within 100 feet of any water body, and identification of unique stream areas for special protection. State-mandated environmental laws, such as wetlands protection and environmental impact review, are included. Zoning categories for commercial, residential, agricultural, and forest uses are established, along with use guidelines and density restrictions, and project review procedures. Subdivision standards apply for five or more lots. Sewage and waste disposal standards are based on a site examination of soil, slope, groundwater, and bedrock characteristics.[11] This code is primarily based on natural land capabilities and area goals described in the CTHPB plan. The Rural Development Code's table of contents and a portion of Part III, Natural Resource Regulations, are presented in Tables 4.3 and 4.4.

Seven towns have so far adopted similar versions of this code. Some differences occur, due to individual community preferences. For example, the town of Osceola identified specific unique stream areas within its town for additional protection.[12] Two towns control lot size; others regulate frontage.

TABLE 4.3

Proposed Rural Development Code, June 1977

TABLE OF CONTENTS	PAGE

TABLE 4.3 (continued)

Proposed Rural Development Code, June 1977

TABLE OF CONTENTS (continued)	PAGE

Source: Cooperative Tug Hill Planning Board.

Five of these towns have joined together to implement the code through an intermunicipal agreement, allowed by New York State law. The agreement includes a joint zoning board of appeals, the first in the state.[13] Several towns share an enforcement officer. The CTHPB has just recruited its own full-time community coordinator.

The six planning boards in towns adopting the code by January 1978 reviewed twenty-eight permit applications during the 1978 building season, a substantial amount of activity in an area with a density of eight persons per square mile. These permits covered a variety of activities, from construction of single family dwellings and mobile homes to changes in commercial use. One subdivision was reviewed and discouraged. In addition, the cooperative enforcement officer acted on code violations relating to malfunctioning sep-

TABLE 4.4

Sample Section of The Cooperative Tug Hill Planning Board's Proposed Rural
Development Code, Part III, Natural Resource Regulations, Articles B and C

Article B: WATER RELATED AREAS

1. Streams, Lakes, Ponds, and Wetlands
   The following regulations apply to all land within 100 feet of these bodies:
   a. Prohibited Activities
      —dumping of waste materials, junk, refuse, or anything that would
      alter the quality of the water, or the character of the area.
      —construction of any principal or accessory use.
      —construction of a public street, or public utility line.
   b. Conditional Activities (requiring a permit)
      —any alteration of the water body, such as impoundment, diversion,
      or excavation.
      —alteration of any existing building.
   c. Compatible Activities (not requiring a permit)
      —existing development.
      —passive recreation.
      —conservation practices.
      —raising crops.
      —pasturing animals, not including feed lots.
2. Wetlands
   Areas shown on DEC maps as official freshwater wetland shall be
   regulated according to the provisions contained in Article 24 of the
   N.Y.S. Environmental Conservation Law including subsequent amend-
   ments, which is adopted herein by reference.
3. Flood Hazard Areas
   These areas are shown by HUD maps and all activity in such areas
   shall conform to the standards contained in the Flood Disaster Protection
   Act of 1973 which is adopted herein by reference.
4. Special Areas
   Areas designated by each town as significant areas of special quality,
   mapped and described in the Resource Management Plan, are protected
   by the following standards. These shall apply to a buffer area of 200
   feet on each side of the designated area. The following activites are
   prohibited in these areas.
      —construction of any principal or accessory use.
      —dumping of junk, waste, etc.
      —cutting of more than 50 percent of volume of timber.

TABLE 4.4 (continued)

The Cooperative Tug Hill Planning Board Natural Resource Regulations

---

Article B: WATER RELATED AREAS (continued)

—mining.
—feed lots.
—landings when possible.
—chemical thinning.
—construction of a public street or utility line.
—transmission lines.

Article C: FOREST MANAGEMENT STANDARDS

The intent of this section is to define minimum standards for all commercial harvesting of timber. Clear-cutting is prohibited except when necessary in special situations. Individuals cutting for home use are also encouraged to follow these standards.

1. General Standards
   —minimize damage to site and remaining vegetation.
   —prevent conditions which increase the chance of forest fire.
   —no hardwood under 12″ DBH or softwood under 10″ DBH should be cut for sawtimber unless deformed, diseased, or removal is necessary for thinning.
   —no hardwood under 10″ DBH or softwood under 6″ DBH should be cut for pulp unless deformed, diseased, or removal is necessary for thinning.
   —all seedling or sapling areas are to be protected from damage caused by logging in adjacent areas.
   —install erosion control measures on logging roads.
   —keep 50 percent of the volume within 100 feet of the centerline of a public right-of-way where possible.
   —clear landings, after use, of man-made debris, e.g., cables, gas cans, tires, etc.
   —encourage the preservation of some cull trees as den trees for wildlife and bees.
2. In order to maintain a protective strip of vegetation within 50 feet of a water body, the following forestry requirements are established:
   —obtain permit from DEC for any water body crossing.
   —winch logs off steep slopes and minimize the number of skid trails.
   —log steep slopes during dry weather or when the ground is frozen.

Source: Cooperative Tug Hill Planning Board, *Model Rural Development Code* (Watertown, N.Y.: June 1977), pp. 32–34.

tic tanks, construction without a permit, stream pollution by loggers, and other issues.[14]

Two specific examples illustrate how this cooperative system functions. In the fall of 1978, the town of West Turin reviewed a subdivision of three relatively expensive houses, with three more planned for future construction, on land then zoned for agricultural use only. The developer made a strong case, based on soil type, for being allowed to construct on this particular parcel. Rather than grant a variance and set a precedent of being easily swayed, the board asked the developer to wait until it revised the boundaries of its agricultural zone to conform with the new soil information. In a case in the town of Florence, a construction permit was denied. This was appealed to the five-town cooperative zoning board of appeals and was resolved satisfactorily.

The intermunicipal agreement is the cement of the present cooperative board. This agreement has been termed "the most important step in welding together the cooperative planning program."[15] Its joint contract formally creates the CTHPB, allows it to spend money, establishes its structure, and, most importantly, grants it a number of powers normally delegated to a regular local planning board. The present partnership was formed in January 1979.

Overall, town boards and planning boards are still pleased with the CTHPB. Some lack of momentum resulted because two towns did not adopt the rural development code, but requests of other towns to join and begin planning under the CTHPB model have balanced this. Town board membership has changed since 1974 in many towns, weakening cooperative planning board support in some towns and increasing it in others. This change is partly due to increased political sophistication in some towns, weakening of old political connections, and cooperative planning board members going on to other town jobs.

From 1975 to 1977, during the most intensive effort, at least three Commission staff people were involved with the CTHPB, as they described it, "in personal, protracted, and intense fashion," and "with 100 percent immersion contact." Besides two planners, the support staff included a rural aide "circuit rider" responsible to the CTHPB and substantial input from the technical assistance program. Technical assistance to planning and town boards in individual towns played a key role in building the capabilities of these towns to continue with planning at the cooperative level with other towns.

The Commission's planning director outlined several points regarding staff handling of this process in a 1979 article. The code and plan were kept as simple as possible, including more explanation of purposes and intent than is common. A wide range of alternatives was presented early on, with final decisions left up to the cooperative planning board. Discussion began with noncontroversial topics to build a base for agreement on more difficult issues. Joint planning also led to the group's desire for joint implementation.[16]

SALMON RIVERS COOPERATIVE PLANNING BOARD: A Joint Plan

The Salmon Rivers Cooperative Planning Board (SRCPB) was formed in May 1976 by three towns and two villages in the western part of the Tug Hill area. A fourth town, Williamstown, joined a year later. This board is often considered to be another example of effective cooperative planning. Although it is a newer organization, the SRCPB has a wider scope of activities than the CTHPB. It also has a different orientation, perhaps most evident in the title of its recently completed areawide plan: "Comprehensive Regional Development Plan," as opposed to CTHPB's "Resource Management Plan."[17]

Geographically and socially, the six SRCPB municipalities are different in several respects. Albion and Parish, the two most populous towns, both contain villages with access to Interstate Route 81. Residential growth is moderately rapid in these two towns, as it is in Orwell. Parish includes more active farmland; the other three towns are slightly more forested. Orwell and Williamstown have many seasonal residents.[18] In recent local planning board meetings, Parish village discussed downtown revitalization, while Orwell considered a five-year road plan and progress on a ski trail network.

Yet all four towns consider recreation pressures, future growth, and employment to be crucial issues.[19] The presence of two state parcels, Chateaugay State Forest and Happy Valley Game Management Area, that lie in all four towns, also gives rise to some intertown concerns. And the SRCPB area encompasses much of the Salmon River watershed, including the site of a new state fish hatchery at Altmar, now nearing completion.

Only Parish town and village had undertaken a previous planning and zoning effort, and it was not a positive experience. The village already had a zoning ordinance, and, in the early 1970s, a joint planning board conducted background studies and prepared a master plan with a county planner's assistance. The plan was not translated into land use controls.

As a reaction to the state's salmon stocking program, which was beginning to bring thousands of fishermen to the Salmon River every fall, and to the planned salmon hatchery in Altmar, the Albion Town Board developed a sudden interest in zoning, both to control fishermen and to attract businesses to serve them.

Thus the cooperative planning board's formation was a combination of local interest in "doing something" and positive response to a Commission presentation on the possible benefits of cooperative planning.

After a few general meetings, the towns of Orwell and Albion and the village of Altmar formed planning boards and then joined Parish in a cooperative group. Parish members appear to have been most interested in long-term watershed protection. Williamstown refused to join then came into the group in the fall of 1977 after a positive experience seeking grant money with the Commission's help and several visits by the SRCPB community coordinator. A similar effort to gain the formal involvement of more conservative Amboy was not successful.

The SRCPB has undertaken a wide range of activities in three and a half years. One major effort has been devoted to preparing a comprehensive plan, including resource inventories, individual and joint goal formulation, two citizen surveys, and public meetings. This group has also emphasized the need for citizen education; it is one of two boards participating in the Commission's special citizen education program. Possible future joint projects may include an areawide landfill or refuse collection site. The SRCPB also gives attention to individual town concerns, particularly for revising local ordinances or introducing new ideas such as site plan review.[20] Further, as part of its simultaneous appointment as a joint Conservation Advisory Council, it conducted a stream inventory, stream water quality sampling, and a wetlands inventory. Responsibility for local project review under the State Environmental Quality Review Act is also delegated to the cooperative board by three of the member towns.

The SRCPB started right off with group projects, and the Commission staff provided impetus and assistance. In the first few months, the SRCPB conducted windshield surveys of each town, wrote a supplementary questionnaire for a county citizen survey, and dicussed concerns related to the salmon hatchery. The board also decided to prepare areawide resource inventories and a master plan. It began the process of agreeing on group goals and objectives, reviewed natural resource information, prepared a budget, and began the search for a rural aide/community coordinator.

A first and most obvious result of these activities was members' education. The SRCPB chairman wrote that "as each study is presented, the members find revealed to them a view of each town which had been unknown or unthought of before. . . . A new comprehensive view of this three-town area begins to be seen. The board is starting to grasp the idea of a real working relationship."[21]

The SRCPB's planning goals are broadranging. They were first prepared by individual local planning boards. Like the CTHPB, this group attempted to balance local and areawide interests by reviewing and discussing goals at both levels. These goals appear to be affirmed by results of the board's 1979 citizen survey of half the area households.[22]

The portion of the plan on land use considers natural resource, social, cultural, and historical factors. In addition, the plan recommends measures for future community facilities and services, transportation, recreational development, and housing. It also includes a separate economic development plan emphasizing the area's natural strengths, especially outdoor recreation potential (see Table 4.5).[23]

Convinced of the importance of citizen education and information, SRCPB members devoted much effort to presenting the plan in their communities. Flyers summarizing the plan went to each house in the area. In addition, radio and newspaper ads announced public meetings on both the plan and background studies.

Interest of Salmon River area citizens in land use planning is hard to measure. While forty people attended a meeting in Orwell on background studies, the four official August 1979 public hearings on the plan drew only forty residents, plus planning board and town board members. Turnout for other workshops connected with the SRCPB citizen education program was also low, despite heavy advertising. Yet the 1979 survey of all residents showed that of the 55 percent responding, two to one favored cooperative planning.

Tug Hill's rolling uplands, with old logging trails and unplowed roads, are ideal for snowmobiling and cross-country skiing. *Photograph courtesy of Roswell P. Trickey*, Watertown *Daily Times*.

TABLE 4.5

Salmon Rivers Cooperative Planning Board Goals and Objectives in 1979 Plan

Maintain high quality environment:	Air and water quality
Encourage local employment opportunities:	Agriculture
	Existing business
	Area strengths
	Transportation location
	Recreation
Maintain and encourage rural life styles:	Land use program
	Growth control
Provide adequate housing	Health and safety
Provide community facilities and services:	Education
	Volunteer services
	Water and sewer supply
Develop adequate transportation	Road maintenance, recreational access, and parking
Preserve cultural heritage	Awareness

Source: Salmon Rivers Cooperative Planning Board, *Comprehensive Regional Development Plan* (Watertown, N.Y.: 1979), pp. 5–8.

The SRCPB has spent comparatively little time designing land use regulations to enforce its plan. The plan considers implementation in general terms. In October 1979, cooperative board members were assigned the task of discussing an acceptable implementation program with the planning board of the towns they represented. Yet one cooperative planning board officer said, "We won't suggest a rural development code, a single law: the town boards won't go for it."

In part, this reflects the SRCPB's stage of the planning process and preference for approaching issues a step at a time. But it also reflects a distinction between planning and land use controls among local planning and town boards. One cooperative board member firmly stated his belief in the need for planning in his town but had doubts about "telling other people what to do with their land."

Contributions from member towns provide part of the support for the cooperative board. The first (1977) budget contained a $400 appropriation from each municipality. In the fall of 1979, all but one local government also approved about $1,500 more for a rural aide's salary after his CETA eligibility ends. Since the cooperative board also serves as a Conservation Advisory Council, the group is eligible, under New York State law, for up to 50 percent reimbursement from the New York State Department of Environmental Conservation for most of its expenses.

This local funding implies a commitment by most of these town and village boards to the cooperative project. In addition, all six local governing boards signed the 1979 intermunicipal agreement with few complaints, as it was taken around by planning board members and Commission staff. The SRCPB chairman terms present town board attitudes "good but untested."[24]

On the other hand, town boards can withdraw support quickly. For example, in 1978 the Albion/Altmar planning board, responding to a town board request, prepared an interim zoning ordinance with Commission help. After two negative public hearings, the town board rejected the zoning ordinance. As a result, "zoning, planning and the Tug Hill Commission are all bad words" in this town; "the Tug Hill Commission got crucified and we got burned." The planning board continued to function, trying to work within an expanded zoning commission that included the vocal opponents to land use laws.

Officers and members of the SRCPB have remained fairly consistent over three and a half years. While membership on one local planning board has changed drastically, the SRCPB chairman and vice-chairman are the same two elected at the first meeting. Local and cooperative planning board members are a mixed group: some are lifelong residents of the area and others are newcomers. Many were previously active politically, if only as observers at town board meetings. As with the CTHPB, individual members became directly involved in conducting surveys, developing citizen education programs, and preparing the plan.

The SRCPB has also received fairly constant assistance from Commission staff. For most of its existence, both a planner and rural aide, and recently a citizen education coordinator, have assisted the group. It has sponsored at least one summer intern of its own for wetlands inventorying. Three different rural aides served in 1979, but SRCPB members did not note this as a major problem. The

SRCPB did not make an official declaration of independence from Commission staff; this independence was assumed from the start.

NORTH SHORE COOPERATIVE PLANNING BOARD:
Technical Assistance

Four towns and two villages comprise the North Shore Cooperative Planning Board (NSCPB). One town is in Oneida County; the rest are in Oswego County. All border the north shore of Oneida Lake, which lies between these towns and Syracuse to the south. The NSCPB was formed in May 1977. Its most recent member, Constantia, joined nearly a year later. These towns are the most populous of the five cooperative planning board areas.

Population growth is occurring in this area, although it is not evenly distributed. In this regard these towns differ markedly from others in the Commission's study area. The southern, or lakeshore, part of each town is valued for suburban development. Growth is heaviest in the two western towns, Hastings and West Monroe.[25] Hastings' land area is nearly 20 percent active agriculture, while Vienna, the easternmost town, is almost half forest. Of the two villages, Central Square, an expanding residential community with more businesses, is situated on Interstate Route 81; Cleveland, fifteen miles away along the lake, is much smaller.

Although each town planning board sees its town as different, with unique character and problems, they also share some common programs, such as an ambulance corps and a senior citizens group. In addition, the lakeshore is a popular site for recreation and second homes for nearby city dwellers as well as local residents.

Since its formation, the NSCPB has primarily served as a forum for airing individual town land use problems and receiving assistance on them. Unlike other cooperative boards, this group has not yet undertaken a joint citizen survey. It has considered natural resource inventories and background studies prepared by Commission staff and has just begun a joint planning effort. Commitments to joint efforts have been arrived at slowly in these towns, in comparison to other cooperative boards.

Much of the NSCPB's work has consisted of reviewing model or local ordinances for specific issues, such as junkyards and trailers, and proposing these to local governing boards through local planning boards. The 1979–80 work program is 40 percent local planning assistance; 30 percent planning board, town board, and citizen education; and 30 percent group background studies.[26]

Commission staff provides a great deal of individual assistance to these towns. For example, Constantia is among the heaviest users of the technical assistance program, particularly for legal advice.

This focus on local planning issues stems partly from varied and extensive past planning and land use regulation experience. All six municipalities formed local planning boards well before the NSCPB; four of these local groups prepared master plans in the 1960s with federal 701 funds. Their experiences, however, were generally negative. Only Hastings and Central Square translated these plans into zoning ordinances. Constantia's first planning board was discharged when it tried to promote zoning; the second planning board formally adopted a consultant's master plan, and "it has sat right on the shelf since then."[27]

Individual planning boards are busy reviewing proposed developments, updating local ordinances, dealing with enforcement problems, and suggesting regulations to cope with specific problems in their communities. The regulatory framework for land use differs in each municipality. A variety of local laws treat land use issues, including sewage disposal laws, trailer ordinances, subdivision regulations, and other single-issue laws in addition to zoning. A Commission staff member reported strong antizoning feelings among town residents, with low value placed on comprehensive planning, even among local planning board members. Yet locally unforeseen "crises" can result in rather rapid attitude changes. A recent subdivision proposal, for example, in Constantia, involving local review under the state's Environmental Quality Review Act Law, has increased the stature of the planning board and public confidence in it.

Motives for joining the NSCPB seem varied for individual communities. The common border on Oneida Lake appears to be a minor concern. Reasons for joining, given by individual boards, included the need to stay on top of new regulations, to update old ordinances for new growth, to know informally and early on what other towns planned, to receive planning assistance, and to avoid county planners that, in one NSCPB member's words, "only pushed county concerns."

Virtually all the six local governing boards were at first suspicious of the Commission and of cooperative planning. One town board member summarized this reluctance: "We wanted to see what the other towns would do; we didn't want to be the only one. Also, we had done much planning; why share it with towns behind us in experience?"

To encourage the cooperative board's formation, the Commission apparently presented the idea to individual planning boards after assisting them on particular local issues through the technical assistance program. After several visits with local governing and planning boards, it organized a series of meetings for local officials that led to the NSCPB. The importance of town board resistance is illustrated by the story of the fourth town's official vote to join: the local planning board waited months to raise the issue for a town board vote until a meeting when the town supervisor, the major objector to the cooperative planning board, was absent.

Attempts to approve a cooperative planning board budget containing a locally contributed share of funds have not fared well. In 1978, only about half the town and village boards appropriated the $200 each requested by their local planning boards. The Commission arranged CETA money for the cooperative rural aide position; even this was at first met by lack of enthusiasm among town boards.

In the fall of 1979, the NSCPB made a major effort to secure local governing board support through a formal intermunicipal agreement creating an official cooperative planning board empowered to spend local funds, and through a two-stage appropriation. As of March 1980, the outcome of this effort had not resulted in full participation. In those towns signing, approval was far from automatic. And not all municipalities approved their $400 share of the operating budget. Even fewer included the $1,666 each for a rural aide in their local budget. Despite these trials, NSCPB has shown recent indications of increased strength.

Commission staffing to the NSCPB has not been uniform. For the first seven months, a planner and community coordinator worked part-time. Then, from December 1977 until November 1979, the NSCPB had the same full-time planner. But no rural aide was available for the organizational aspects of this group's work until June 1979.

The Commission's technical assistance staff has provided much individual aid to partly fill this gap. A major example is the Constantia planning board's recent consideration of the first subdivision qualifying for local SEQR review. Commission staff helped the town planning board meet legal requirements, decide what the environmental impact statement should contain, review technical aspects of the draft impact statement, hold all necessary public hearings, and document its decisions adequately in case of a lawsuit. The Commission staff view this as a successful effort to assist in strengthening the planning board's role in the community.

JEFFERSON COUNTY SNOWBELT COOPERATIVE PLANNING BOARD: Citizen Education

The Jefferson County Snowbelt Cooperative Planning Board (JCSB), formed in November 1977, is the smallest cooperative planning board, with only three member towns. It is also the smallest in land area. But it is certainly not the least active.

Adams town and village differ from the towns of Lorraine and Rodman, which are more rural. Three-quarters of Adams' 4,300 people live in the village; a sizeable number are newcomers, often with new ideas about how to run the town. Agriculture is significant in all three towns, although Lorraine is somewhat more forested. Substantial state and county acreage exists in both Lorraine and Rodman. Interstate 81 runs through the village of Adams. All three towns also have seasonal camps. Major local issues include maintaining a healthy agriculture, guiding the increase in residential development, promoting tourism and local business expansion, and deciding how best to draw on natural resources.[28]

Planning boards had been formed, prior to 1973, in all three towns. Adams and Lorraine prepared master plans in the 1960s with federal 701 funds. Both towns had a bad experience, and neither town adopted a zoning ordinance as a result. The proposed zoning ordinance prepared by the consultant for Adams referred to golf courses, building codes, and airport zones. The town planning board struggled to rewrite it for years. Adams village, not a JCSB member because it is so different in character, has its own planning board and zoning ordinance.

This cooperative planning board's formation is partly a result of interest expressed by local officials. A September 1977 meeting of southern Jefferson County local officials was sponsored by the Rodman town supervisor, who was very favorable toward the Commission as a result of technical assistance for a new town water supply system.

Common issues were raised at the meeting, such as possible future expansion of Fort Drum, a nearby military training site, proposed 765 kv transmission lines through the area, preservation of local agricultural lands, and upcoming hearings on state wetlands regulations. In addition, the Commission presented what it saw as the benefits of cooperative planning. Two months later, the cooperative planning board was formed. As one JCSB member put it, "We knew we were being pressed by someone to plan—this way we get to live with it." All three towns signed an intermunicipal agreement in 1979 enabling the cooperative planning board to undertake official actions.

The JCSB's first activities mixed group efforts and local concerns. The board reviewed natural resource information and background studies prepared by Commission staff. JCSB members conducted windshield surveys and surveyed citizen and student opinions on various issues in the three towns. A public meeting considered formation of a local agricultural district and reviewed state wetlands maps.[29]

In a March 1979 essay, the JCSB chairman described the board's purpose: "The role of this board is to maintain a liaison between the three individual town planning boards. Each town has its own business to attend to, and the cooperative board provides technical assistance and information which the individual town might not have access to."[30]

Much of the JCSB's recent effort has been directed toward an extensive areawide citizen education program, including public workshops, activities in local schools, newspaper and radio essays, and a drive-it-yourself tour of the three towns. Individual town concerns are also aired at cooperative planning board meetings. Commission staff also provide direct planning assistance to individual towns.

Areawide cooperative planning was not, until recently, a JCSB activity. It has now approved a joint sketch plan, however, and an

Workshops for teachers in the South Jefferson School District covered how to use planning materials in the classroom.

areawide land use plan is being prepared. An areawide solid waste disposal group was also recently formed through the JCSB.

But joint enforcement of cooperatively developed land use regulations may be a long way from now, even if the board assigns it a top priority. One Adams resident attributed this difference to desires for town independence and to differing town concerns with the long-term future.

The JCSB obtained part of its 1978 and 1979 operating budget through member towns' contributions of $400 each. Commission planning aid has been virtually continuous. The rural aide position has been filled since early 1979, and a Commission staff member coordinates this part of the citizen education project. The planner is currently provided through a joint arrangement with the Black River-St. Lawrence Regional Planning and Development Board. In addition, the Jefferson County Planning Department has recently joined in the area study on solid waste disposal options.

NORTHEAST ONEIDA PLANNING BOARD: A Loose Federation

The newest cooperative planning board, the Northeast Oneida Planning Board (NEON), was envisioned as far back as the fall of 1975. A Commission-sponsored meeting of informal representatives from six Oneida County towns in the Tug Hill area agreed on the need to work together in planning matter and set a priority on Commission aid to towns with no comprehensive plans.[31] But the cooperative board did not officially form until August 1978. As of spring 1980, NEON was a loose federation, without an intermunicipal agreement uniting it or local funds appropriated to it. It is the only group that did not choose the word "cooperative" for its title.

The four current members of NEON are all within commuting distance of Rome and Utica. Three towns already have many new suburban residents, and expect further moderate to rapid future growth. The fourth town, Steuben, has more agricultural and state land. Lee also contains some farmlands. The presence of Griffiss Air Force Base raises land use issues for several of these towns. At least three towns see themselves primarily as bedroom communities, not part of Tug Hill. They do not see much in common with each other.

Planning and regulation experience in these four towns is quite varied. Steuben received assistance in preparing its 1978 town plan and citizen survey from both the Tug Hill Commission and Oneida-Herkimer Comprehensive Planning Program.[32] Floyd, on the other hand, has an established planning board comprised partly of long-term, older affluent residents, a comprehensive town plan, a zoning ordinance, and subdivision regulations. In 1979, its zoning board of appeals considered nine separate requests. At least three towns have received planning assistance from Oneida County in response to individual requests.

Motives for this board's formation by town boards are not clear. Town boards do not appear threatened by NEON or to oppose its existence. NEON, however, operates primarily as a discussion group. It has undertaken no common projects, though it has considered a citizen survey. Three of the four town boards completed separate town plans and thus are not interested in the background studies that formed a large part of other cooperative boards' early activities. One issue three of the towns share is updating their zoning

Towns in the southern rim, close to cities, are experiencing rapid growth.
Photograph courtesy of W. H. Kennedy, Jr.

ordinances in response to a recent Griffiss Air Force Base plan. But
they are approaching this individually.

The NEON planner provides much valuable day-to-day advice
to the cooperative and local planning boards. This person also aids in
revising local ordinances and providing information to local boards,
and has organized training sessions on topics of potential group
interest. Town interest in individual assistance is high.

But interest in cooperative planning lags on this board. Many
local planning board representatives are reluctant to participate.
NEON did not meet during winter 1979–80, and its April 1980
meeting was poorly attended. Efforts to reach other local officials
involved in land use issues, such as town clerks and enforcement
officers, have been largely unsuccessful. One NEON meeting on
SEQR was well attended, however.[33]

NEON has regrouped at least twice, to better define its role and
seek suitable organizational framework to keep it functioning. Only

Steuben appears highly positive toward cooperative planning; this is largely due to satisfaction with planning and technical assistance received by the town from the Commission.

NEON has been able to obtain the least Commission staff assistance of any cooperative planning board. One Commission staff member pointed to this inability to deliver promised services, after actively generating local interest, as a major factor in NEON's poor performance. First, due to recruitment difficulties, a full-time planner was not provided to the board until June 1979. This planner is jointly shared with the Oneida County Planning Department, a group the towns in this area are more familiar with. Second, a rural aide has never been involved with NEON, due to lack of county approval of a CETA-financed position, and so organizational aid is not extensive. And, except for Steuben, NEON towns have been infrequent users of the Commission's technical assistance program, so there have been few visible results to point to. NEON has, till now, been an unsuccessful experiment in cooperative planning. However, if some towns find a use for NEON, this situation might change.

THE UNCOMMITTED TOWNS

As of March 1980, thirteen towns and fifteen villages in the Commission's study area were not involved with Commission programs as cooperative planning board members. This is not necessarily a negative reflection on the Commission. This is, after all, a voluntary program; while the Commission may encourage, it cannot require, local involvement.

Not all towns and villages want outside help; others receive this help from other sources. Some municipalities, such as Camden and Boonville, had developed land use plans and controls on their own, often through the federal 701 program. While enforcement may present a problem for these local governments, there is a sense of accomplishment in having adopted these controls ahead of other Tug Hill towns. In part, some fringe towns see the Commission's purpose as helping core area towns that cannot plan on their own.

Other towns were motivated to individual action by the Commission's presence. Some of these towns, for example Lewis, are now eager to join cooperative boards, after observing their neighbors' experience. Still other towns feel that they obtain sufficient planning assistance from their county planning board. Increasingly, this help is being coordinated with Commission programs.

Another group of towns and villages do not perceive outside pressures on their lands or do not turn to planning and land use regulation as the answer to these pressures. In agricultural areas, for example, the formation of county-level agricultural districts may be seen as a preferred alternative.

Some towns are opposed to Commission involvement in their local affairs. For a number of local officials, the real issue is distrust of state interference in any form, suspicion of losing local control, or opposition to land use controls at any level of government.

Finally, limitations on Commission staff resources led to emphasis on those towns most open to Commission assistance. Either no strong effort at developing contact was made with other towns, or lack of response after an initial contact, coupled with full commitment of Commission resources elsewhere, led to this situation.

The technical assistance program has not been popular with municipalities that are not members of cooperative planning boards. For example, of the 125 requests received from January to July 1979, only 8 were from towns and villages outside cooperative boards, despite the Commission's apparent willingness to answer questions from these local governments.

Recent workshops on the Commission's transition for local officials sparked a flurry of interest in towns previously uninvolved in Commission programs.[34] For example, a request was received from Lowville village about the possibility of planning assistance to update its zoning ordinance. This led to a meeting of the Commission, the Black River-St. Lawrence Regional Planning staff, and five municipalities in the northeastern Tug Hill area to discuss forming a cooperative board and providing it with services.

In summary, uninvolved towns and villages have different characteristics and different reasons for their nonparticipation. But many of them tend to have one or more of the following characteristics: substantial and positive past experience with planning, higher populations with larger numbers of suburban residents, and strong do-it-themselves attitudes. At the same time, fewer villages tend to participate and fewer strongly agricultural towns. While generaliza-

Planner works with Osceola Planning Board on map overlays to show the interaction between natural resources and the activities of man.

tions are difficult, cooperative planning boards have appeared to work better in towns with relatively small amounts of agricultural activity, small, sparsely distributed populations, and few nonfarm economic activities—towns that, not surprisingly, need the help most.

5 The Commission's Impact: Significant Accomplishments

EVALUATION: From Whose Perspective?

AN EVALUATION of a state commission's achievements, strengths, and weaknesses must recognize the existence of differing perspectives on its activities. The presence of a state commission is an additional factor in governmental and private decision-making for the affected area. The Commission will be judged differently depending upon the interests and expectations of the groups it affects.

Several groups are potentially affected by Tug Hill Commission activities: those directly involved in its programs, primarily local planning board members; local elected officials in the Tug Hill area; and Tug Hill citizens. Also affected are county governments, regional agencies, the state government, and other outside interests. These groups judge the Commission from at least two differing perspectives: (1) the view that regional natural resource protection should result from such a Commission; and (2) the view that local capacity building should result.

Disappointment with the Commission actions is most common among those groups and individuals who desire stronger state action to protect the area, who expect a regional plan, or who prefer more emphasis on areawide economic issues. There are also those who object to state interference in the area or oppose local planning or land use regulation in general, and so criticize the Commission's program.

The Tug Hill Commission itself feels that it has, on the whole, effectively served the area. The Commission's director in a recent article listed several benefits of cooperative planning: (1) an areawide perspective emerges, as local governments make decisions for the good of the entire area; (2) communities talk to each other, and work less at cross purposes; (3) personnel are shared in a cost-effective manner; (4) greater resources are attracted to the area; (5) towns have more influence with the county and state; (6) land use regulations are more consistently enforced; and (7) shared responsibility for decisions reduces political pressure at the local level.[1]

But these benefits are most clearly seen from the perspective that favors local capacity building. This perspective is most common, of course, among local groups. Several issues arise, as identified in Chapter 1, when state-level perspectives are taken into account. How well has the Commission balanced state, local, and outside interests? How has it managed potential conflict of goals among these groups? How has it used its powers to build a political base and to satisfy state-level accountability? And how has the definition of the Tug Hill study area affected the Commission's functioning?

In addition to these considerations, evaluation of the Commission must also consider long-term prospects for continuing its programs.[2] What services of this agency should be continued? What alternatives exist for providing them, and who will bear the cost? And since many indications of the Commission's success may not be apparent for some time, how should success be evaluated in 1985 or 1990?

SUCCESS MEASURES: Local Perspectives

CHANGING VIEWS AT THE LOCAL LEVEL

With some important exceptions, local attitudes toward the Tug Hill Commission and activities it encourages have improved since the agency's formation.[3] Many planning board members and local elected officials, especially in towns and villages participating in Commission programs, are positive about the Commission's role and their experience. Initial hostility of many Tug Hill citizens evident at the 1974 public forums is apparently much reduced and presently exists in only a few areas. One Cooperative Extension agent noted that in his county, "Opposition to the Commission comes almost exclusively from a few misinformed or uninvolved towns." Attitudes toward local planning, land use control, and the need for outside assistance have also changed. Wary citizens still distrust the more distant (and abstract) state presence.

Positive local attitudes toward the Commission are most obvious among cooperative planning board members, those most directly in contact with Commission staff. These individuals, for the most part, view favorably their experience as board members and experience with Commission programs. Those interviewed in four of five cooperative board areas were, almost without exception, highly enthusiastic about the importance of their board's work to their communities and about the usefulness of Commission assistance.[4]

For example, several of the most active cooperative board members, particularly in the core area, were at first suspicious of the Commission as a representative of the state and opposed to town land use planning or controls. Now many of these people speak highly of the Commission's approach.

Cooperative planning board members commonly gave several reasons for this supportive attitude: the need for such assistance, the service-oriented approach of the staff, the highly educational experience of sitting on a board, and, for some, the importance of intertown cooperation on land use issues. In addition, cooperative planning board members often view their town's problems in the long term. The Commission enabled them to promote this view in their communities.

Local technical assistance provided by Commission staff is a major factor in support of the Commission. Some interviewees pointed to land use planning aid; others emphasized legal advice, organization, help with specific local issues, or the role of a rural aide. Several had tried unsuccessfully to obtain similar assistance from their county. The dominant feeling at the November 1979 workshops on the Commission's future was that without continuing assistance, cooperative and even local planning boards will find their work much more difficult.[5]

Another reason for enthusiasm is the perception that Commission staff supports a local board's right to make its own decisions and does not force any one viewpoint. Several cooperative board members interviewed noted a real "let us help you attitude," described by one cooperative board chairman as "totally unbiased assistance." This point was also raised at the 1979 workshops. And one board member in a town originally reluctant to join a cooperative group feels the Commission staff would have provided aid anyway, even if the town decided not to join. This defense of Commission staff and its approach extends even to situations where planning board work was locally rejected and local governing boards accused the Commission of interference.

In addition, cooperative board members have clearly learned a great deal; this contributes to their satisfaction. Both conversations with them and review of their work to date are evidence of this. Finally, support for the concept of intertown planning, with its potential as a forum for discussing issues that transcend local boundaries, figures heavily in satisfaction of a few cooperative board participants. However, others see cooperative planning primarily as a vehicle for needed local assistance, and a few believe that cooperative intentions have failed in their area, even though a formal board exists.

Most cooperative board members separate themselves, their decisions, and their local concerns from those of the Commission and the state. Some recall the use of scare tactics by the Commission, such as threats of greater state interference in local affairs, in prompting towns to join cooperative boards. For example, one cooperative planning board officer half jokingly described his town's motives for involvement, "If I'm going to have a state tyrant, I'd rather it be a local one, so I can sit in his yard and talk to him."

In short, most cooperative planning board members, both past and present, strongly support Commission programs and are highly satisfied with the Commission's work in their community. This includes influential local individuals who were originally mistrustful of the Commission and representatives of towns at first hostile to its presence.

Has the Tug Hill Commission won over other local government officials with equal success? The evidence is mixed but on the whole positive. A number of local elected officials view Commission programs favorably, especially in contrast with earlier attitudes. Yet many local governing board members lack adequate knowledge of just what the Commission has done. This is true at least in part because governing board members are often not familiar with day-to-day activities of their local planning boards and thus of the Commission. Town membership on a cooperative planning board does not guarantee support for the board's activities.

It is easy to see why those local officials who support Commission programs do so. The programs have provided tangible results for municipalities, through grant assistance and improved planning and other services. Some towns, for example, favor the Commission because they feel it is more responsive to their planning needs than the county. At the same time, the Commission has not directly threatened local governments or advocated a reduction of their power. The town of Adams, for example, was at first mistrustful of the Commission's intentions but is now an active member of a cooperative planning board. Further, the Commission actively sought advice of local government officials in forming its 1976 policy recommendations.[6]

By and large, it is the technical assistance program that impresses town and village board members. For example, while the supervisor of one North Shore town was negative toward the NSCPB, he praised the technical assistance program. Staff help with technical, legal, planning, zoning, and other issues was the most frequent Commission function mentioned at the November 1979 workshops on the Commission's future. At these same meetings, the staff's personal touch and service-oriented approach were often mentioned.

Weak regional unity in the Tug Hill area has contributed to lack of concern among many local officials for the Commission's research and recommendations on regionwide issues. But some core area local officials perceive a new clout with counties and the state through their cooperative planning board.

Yet the staff's success in winning over local elected officials is far from complete. One area Cooperative Extension agent, noting that many town officials are neutral about the Commission's continuation, senses behind this a latent negative attitude. Some local governments, including members of some cooperative planning boards, are still suspicious that the Commission might take over local powers. One Oswego County official observed, "The Commission has tried to pose as something other than a state agency, but they haven't fooled anyone; towns were suspicious then, and they still are." Two core area town officials noted that their town boards still see the state trying to force "APA (Adirondack Park Agency) through the back door" with this Commission.

In short, reaction of many local officials to Tug Hill Commission programs has changed over eight years, from negative suspicion to a positive sense that some of their needs have been met. On the other hand, a sizeable number are not familiar enough with Commission activities to voice an informed judgment. Other local officials, while officially positive or neutral, do not in practice support the Commission's continuation.

Citizen opinion about the Tug Hill Commission's achievements, apart from those in local government, appears to be mixed. Some actively support the Commission, but changes are difficult to generalize. In many communities, including some belonging to cooperative planning boards, there is little awareness of the Commission and its activities. And in some towns there is still a latent fear of state interference.

Some people, particularly in fringe communities, have become supporters of the Commission's focus on environmental issues and planning. But for those who were concerned to begin with, the sense of crisis prompted by the Horizon proposal has died down. A few people expected more emphasis on economic development; these people are disappointed in the Commission's work. Generally speaking, however, most citizens who are aware of the Tug Hill Commission apparently feel it has satisfied some area needs. But, as one cooperative planning board member put it, "very few would have an opinion." A member of this person's town board commented, "There are those in this town against it. But they don't understand the Commission. There's a lack of knowledge in this town." One commissioner evaluated the agency's performance this way: "Apparently the Commission isn't resented, but I suspect there is not much interest in or knowledge of our work."

And even in cooperative planning board towns with extensive citizen education programs, awareness of the Commission's role appears low. This lack of knowledge is reflected in numerous participant comments at the November 1979 workshops identifying a lack of local resident awareness of the Commission and its activities. Some criticized the Commission for being too low-key in its publicity.

Among those who are informed about the Commission, according to one Cooperative Extension agent, many find it hard to see precisely what the Commission's impacts are. There is a pervading sense among many knowledgeable Tug Hill citizens that the Commission has involved towns with previously low interest in land use issues. But, except for recognizing dramatic examples, much of this success is perceived as limited to the isolated core area.

At the same time, no substantial vocal opposition exists within the area to the Commission or its programs. Occasional negative comments are heard, particularly about state bureaucracy and loss of home rule. For example, the Lewis County Farm Bureau passed a 1977 resolution opposing the Commission.

But the lack of active citizen opposition is most clearly evidenced by statements of local legislators. Senator Barclay's active support of the Commission is largely attributable to the views of his constituents. He feels the majority of residents with an opinion on the Commission have a favorable one. Assembly member H. Robert Nortz reports a few dissidents, primarily individuals or towns who have never participated in Commission programs. Senator Barclay has heard a few complaints but no substantive criticisms. Former assembly member Donald L. Taylor heard no complaints during his term of service.[7]

In summary, there is little active opposition in the Tug Hill area to the Commission and its activities. Further, most groups directly involved with the Commission are strongly supportive. The outright hostility originally facing the agency has apparently disappeared. More importantly, most local elected officials are at least neutral, and often positive, toward the Commission's work.

IMPACTS ON LOCAL DECISION-MAKING

Cooperative Planning

The Commission has clearly increased the number and effectiveness of local governments undertaking some form of the planning process in the Tug Hill area. It has assisted more than thirty towns and villages, many with little or no previous planning experience, to form or strengthen their local planning boards and to work on some aspect of local planning or land use management. It has primarily done this through fostering the formation of cooperative planning boards.

Establishment of these cooperative planning boards through intermunicipal agreements is an unusual contribution to improving local land use planning capability. But existence of these boards is only one, perhaps not the most significant, impact of the Commission's efforts. The activities of these boards, whom they influence, and the strength of their contacts with town and village governing boards are important secondary impacts of the Commission's activities.

One clear result is a core of enthusiastic and well-informed cooperative planning board members. Another is that local planning programs are now professionally staffed. Beyond this, results vary by community. Each sees different results, though almost none see no benefits at all. Individual cooperative planning boards have made mixed progress in their efforts, and local involvement gaps in cooperative planning exist.

The five cooperative planning boards differ markedly in several respects: progress to cooperative plans, land use regulations and enforcement; sense of group purpose and motivations for formation; and support from town boards and community residents. The CTHPB, the first board formed, is the most successful on these counts. But its members are an unusual group of towns. The SRCPB, with different goals and different member towns, is also successful in terms of motivation, activities, and local support. At the time of this review, NEON was not functioning effectively, while NSCPB was undergoing change toward somewhat increased effectiveness.

These differences result from many factors, only some of them related to Commission approach and activities. Motives for joining a cooperative board, expectations of its work, and commitment to cooperative land use planning vary. Not all cooperative groups work on land use planning; some fill a need for other kinds of communication among towns. A sense of crisis, or lack of it, associated with a board's formation goes a long way to explaining town board support of cooperative programs.

Other factors contributing to differences in cooperative board effectiveness are the degree of past county assistance available to the community, and financial and other limits to governmental resources. Towns with limited governmental resources and those unable to get planning assistance from the county are most likely to embrace cooperative planning. In addition, those Tug Hill area towns with less prior planning and zoning experience have had an easier time accepting local planning and working with other communities toward joint goals. This may be a result of lack of interest in joint planning by towns that were already actively involved in planning programs on their own.

The degree of subregional identity among communities in a cooperative group also influences its success. Some member towns do not see common interests or social identity with other communities in their group as strongly as others do. Further, those towns with higher population, more agricultural lands, and more local businesses seem to look less positively on intertown cooperation. A poor sense of group identity, combined with the absence of a crisis demanding immediate attention, appears to be a factor in the slower performance of at least two cooperative boards.

If one takes a broad view of planning, then the activities of all cooperative boards fall under this heading. But different cooperative groups are clearly working toward different goals. This contributes to some confusion as to the purpose of cooperative planning, beyond receiving local assistance. Nevertheless, cooperative boards have improved numerous local ordinances, given attention to economic development, provided some public education, and in some cases improved links between local planning boards and town boards. One former CTHPB member, somewhat discouraged, asked: "What have we done? Not much." He then described the rural development code, his own education, increased awareness of his neighbors about land use issues, a change in his town board for land use planning, and a sense of greater local control.

Links between cooperative planning boards and member planning boards are good, largely because two members of each local board make up the cooperative board. But links between local planning boards and their town boards deserve special comment, for the strength of these links varies greatly. One cooperative planning board chairman remarked that his town board members "don't realize how much is involved in the work we've done for them." In some towns, governing board members may underestimate the contribution of the local cooperative planning boards to their work or may not fully utilize the help they can provide.

Local Land Use Regulations

One major focus of Commission activity over the past eight years has been to encourage local governments in designing, implementing, and enforcing local land use regulations. One result is an innovative rural development code[8] adopted by seven of the participating CTHPB towns and enforced for five towns through an intermunicipal agreement which includes a joint zoning board of appeals. No other cooperative planning board has developed such a code.

However, with extensive individual assistance from the Commission, at least twenty-two other town and village planning boards have completed or are designing or revising at least one local land use ordinance. These efforts range from standard comprehensive zoning codes to building codes, trailer and junkyard ordinances, and site plan review. Most of those completed so far have been adopted. Others are still being prepared. In 1974, less than 20 percent of the towns and villages in the Commission's study area had adopted any form of land use ordinance.[9]

As a direct result of Commission efforts, thirty-nine Tug Hill municipalities chose to adopt local wetlands ordinances to implement the state Freshwater Wetlands Act in advance of a 1976 state deadline for local adoption.[10] Other environmental protection ordinances are less common in the Tug Hill area; the Commission hopes that communities will build these into comprehensive rural development codes. The Commission has also assisted in the adoption of interim land use regulations in towns such as Montague, which approved a forty-two acre minimum lot size to protect its forest lands until its rural development code was in place.[11]

These efforts at land use regulation have increased local confidence in coping with land use issues in some towns and, by example, encouraged other towns to undertake regulation. For the CTHPB area, the rural development code contributes to more consistency in land use regulation across town lines and possibly discourages irresponsible development proposals. Individual regulations for many other communities are tailored to the specific needs of that particular town or village. By organizing into cooperative groups, these small rural towns may be able to better influence major permit decisions of state agencies such as DEC and to force a fuller consideration of the impacts of major developments.

But the results of the Commission's assistance in developing land use ordinances have some limitations. For one, the innovative intertown rural development code is limited to the seven towns that have adopted it. Other cooperative groups presently show little interest in joint land use regulations and enforcement. Instead, much effort is toward ordinances for specific problems, such as junkyards, rather than comprehensive land use regulation.

By tailoring ordinances to individual situations, the Commission is giving local communities the services they want, rather than forcing comprehensive planning. Many towns with previous planning and regulatory experience are not interested in a simple package of ordinances, but rather in strengthening weak spots in their own regulatory system. Local residents in some towns, still suspicious of state intervention, are not likely to adopt outsiders' recommendations. Further development pressures and their effects on attitudes toward land use regulation vary throughout this area. Yet a tradeoff results between tailoring assistance to particular needs and fostering a comprehensive approach.

Interest in land use regulation, especially in the thinly populated towns, may surprise some observers of the rural scene who may feel inclined to attribute this to manipulation by a Commission staff with these goals in mind. That Commission staff members may have tailored their assistance—perhaps subtly—toward such goals cannot be denied. But there is also plenty of evidence that wary Tug Hill townsfolk, suspicious of state intervention, were not likely to "buy" regulatory proposals they did not want. In any event, whether the Commission can be characterized as "pushing" the regulatory approach or not, it is also clear that not all Tug Hill communities are adopting land use regulations; only some, for their own purposes, are. It is not clear what effect this lack of consistency will have on future areawide land use in the Tug Hill area.

It is uncertain whether enforcement of these land use regulations, however thorough they appear on paper, will be as strong as the regulations themselves, especially when the Commission is no longer around to act as a political backstop for unpopular decisions.

the locally oriented zoning board of appeals for a small
~~~ay be lenient with its neighbors and tough on outsiders
~ CTHPB enforcement record so far shows that in at least
~~~~~ ~~~~~, such is not the case.[12] The CTHPB supports local enforcement, partly through a joint enforcement officer; this support is
not a factor in other cooperative areas. The Commission has made
some efforts to prepare local governments for enforcement responsibilities, but these may not be enough.

A final question regarding these regulations is their actual effect
on shaping growth and land use, particularly in handling large-scale
development. This land use regulatory system has not yet been fully
tested by a major development proposal. For example, how would
the CTHPB react if Georgia Pacific at some future date sold
much of its core area acreage for second home development? Such
large-scale developments are most likely to be isolated proposals
with long intervals between them. Although it appears that this local
system in combination with existing state regulations can influence
such proposals, changes in the membership of the boards charged
with enforcing it over these long intervals are likely. Only time will
tell whether the present system can retain its sharpness and expertise
in dealing with such challenges. This system evolved, in part,
assuming the lack of such large-scale immediate development pressures; its functioning under economic conditions that encourage
rapid growth is a major unknown.

Strengthening Local Government Capability

The Tug Hill Commission has made some important contributions to strengthening local government capabilities and confidence
in the Tug Hill area. These contributions include: improved services
and assistance to area local governments; education and training of
planning board members, town boards, and area citizens; attraction
of financial assistance to the area; better links between some town
planning boards and their town boards; and, for members of several
cooperative planning boards, increased cooperation and shared responsibilities. These effects are limited to towns involved in Commission programs.

Participating rural local governments have received improved services through several Commission programs, including a technical assistance service, training programs for officials and employees, aid in organization for planning, and rural aides. These have strengthened some local governments by providing advice not previously available, improving governmental organization, and increasing local government awareness of land use issues. Towns that have only recently begun to participate in cooperative programs are just beginning to share in these benefits.

The Commission's extensive technical assistance program, encompassing a wide variety of subjects and techniques, is largely responsible for some local governments' increased ability to manage their affairs. Individual assistance, combined with training sessions and other techniques, has clearly gone a long way to servicing previously unmet needs. It has also resulted in positive attitudes of many local officials toward the Commission, and in participation of some towns in cooperative planning.

Improvements in local management in some cases are dramatic. For example, aid to the small town of Montague helped put its finances in the black by restructuring its finance methods and collecting money available to it from state and federal governments. Montague's town supervisor says, "When we needed them, they were always there."

And most elected officials who use the service are highly positive about the role of technical assistance in enabling them to do their job. One town board member said, "Now we're on the pulse of many new regulations beforehand. The state doesn't send information. We could get a lot of information from others to keep us up to date, but we don't."

The Commission has attracted financial assistance to the area, much of it previously inaccessible to local governments, through grants received from the state and federal agencies and private foundations. It has also acted as a channel for state money to the area through its annual budget appropriations. A recent $25,000 grant to the Commission from the National Science Foundation, for example, represents the first such public education grant to a land use commission. In addition, the Commission has aided at least twenty-one communities in the complicated process of preparing their own successful grant proposals for local CETA projects. And the shared personnel and access to Commission services can be a practical way of delivering services, reducing local costs, and more efficiently using scarce resources.

Since the Commission has emphasized the role of planning boards in its assistance programs, the advantages of Commission programs are most evident in municipalities with good links to their planning boards. As we have seen, working relationships between planning boards and their local governing boards are not uniformly strong. Perhaps a third of these planning boards have experienced serious difficulties with local governing board support. Planning board members' comments ranged from "the town board doesn't understand the planning board's work" to "the town board never asks for anything."

Some of these new planning boards have yet to build trust with their governing board. But more importantly, town boards have not been through the Commission's extensive educational process. Until direct technical assistance to some town boards by rural aides was recently initiated, along with training sessions and occasional meetings, local governing boards had little contact with the Commission and its programs. This can weaken the results of many Commission efforts.

Not all Tug Hill towns and villages have participated in Commission programs, as previously noted. But measuring the Commission's impact directly by the number of municipalities involved is somewhat misleading, as some communities need this assistance more than others, and the program is voluntary. Nonetheless, the Commission's efforts have not substantially strengthened local government capability in all Tug Hill towns, and several small rural towns have received almost no Commission assistance.

There is always the danger that programs to serve local governments, rather than strengthening their capabilities, may build up a dependence on the services provided and become a crutch for some town officials. Without analyzing specific cases, it is not possible to fully address this concern. But three things seem clear: one, some service is necessary for at least some Tug Hill towns to function at current levels of capability; two, this particular program strives to strengthen rather than weaken local problem solving and decision-making abilities; and three, town officials rather than Commission staff turn information into town actions.

Breaching Rural Communication Barriers

In rural areas many factors, such as distance and the tendency for strong home rule, combine to make communication among rural local governments difficult. Yet many issues benefit from group action. Commission activities have helped some towns and villages, especially in the core area, to breach these barriers and to improve both formal and informal lines of communication.

Previous intertown cooperation in the Tug Hill area, as in many other rural areas, was limited to a few instances of informal contact and sharing on concrete problems such as snow removal. Now, as a result of Commission efforts, some communities can discuss both individual and areawide aspects of land use issues, such as trailer regulation and solid waste disposal. Cooperative planning boards are an unusual but apparently effective means of getting local governments, through their planning boards, to work together on some issues. In addition, for the CTHPB, shared responsibilities of administering the rural development code strengthen the resolve of individual towns to live up to it.

Equally important is the informal communication that is fostered. Some communities now talk to each other, where they rarely did before. One North Shore town board member explained, "Now we have some unity; we can see what our neighbors are doing." With such information available, towns may, in the future, work less at cross purposes with one another, particularly regarding local land use decisions on community borders. An increased awareness of the broader impacts of many local decisions, not just in land use control, may also develop.

Another result of Commission programs has been improved links between the area's local governments and higher-level institutions. Tug Hill municipalities did not have strong institutional links to broader society.[13] For example, representation on existing county and regional planning boards is not high. Bringing local governments together can provide these groups with a formal mechanism for exerting influence on county- and state-level decisions and for making their needs known. For example, the CTHPB lobbied strongly in 1979, through state legislative representatives, for state legislation to reform road abandonment procedures; this legislation passed.[14] Even a joint letterhead provides a simple but effective means of communicating with the county and state.

This breakdown of rural communication barriers is limited, however, by the number of municipalities participating in cooperative programs, by the effectiveness of individual cooperative boards in bringing towns and villages together, and by the existence and effectiveness of the Commission's rural aide. The Commission has not explored the possibility of establishing a direct connection between local elected officials, through formation of a Tug Hill council of governments or similar organization. But, in any case, some new lines of rural communication have been established and successfully tested in the Tug Hill area.

Education and Involvement of Citizens

Throughout its operation, the Commission has made a substantial effort to involve and inform Tug Hill citizens about cooperative programs and the needs it perceives for this area. This effort has had two substantial results: a small group of educated citizens, primarily on cooperative planning boards, who are versed in land use issues and the workings of local government, and a somewhat increased awareness of area citizens about land use issues, concentrated in cooperative planning areas.

The Commission has tried to communicate with Tug Hill citizens and to upgrade their level of information by several methods, including fostering a high degree of citizen involvement in the planning process and in Commission programs, close work with individual municipalities, publicity on areawide issues, and citizen education programs. These activities have the added benefits of developing a support base within the area for Commission programs and present and future local land use activities.

It appears that the local planning and decision-making process is now open to larger numbers of citizens. For example, a survey of core area residents indicated that 20 percent had attended a public planning meeting.[15] Many cooperative planning board members throughout the Tug Hill area had been previously uninvolved in local government; several have since gone on to elective positions. At least in the core area, cooperative planning apparently contributed to opening up old, closed local political systems.

Cooperative planning board members have received most of the benefits of this emphasis on education. Those interviewed viewed this as one of the greatest benefits of involvement in cooperative planning programs. These individuals are now well versed in both the organization and process of local government, as well as in natural resource and land use issues.

Assessing the general educational impact of Commission programs on Tug Hill citizens is nearly impossible. Some citizens education programs, in the JCSPB and SRCPB areas, drew low turnouts and, by some cooperative planning board members' estimates, had little impact. But throughout this report, changes in attitude of local officials and citizens about land use issues and planning are noted. While this impact varies between areas with and without cooperative planning boards, it is clear that some attitudes have changed. Perhaps the strongest evidence of a successful educational effort is that many more local governments actively participate in land use management than before.

No one agency can reach everyone through citizen involvement programs. There is a substantial difference, however, between following the format of citizen involvement and actually achieving it. The vast majority of those interviewed feel that the Commission has achieved real participation of Tug Hill citizens. One person familiar with the SRCPB summed it up, "The Tug Hill Commission got more people working than any other agency."

The entire Tug Hill Commission program can be seen, from one perspective, as an educational strategy to prompt change in these rural communities. As one Commission staff member described it, "The Commission is involved in value change. This doesn't happen fast." Indeed, the major limit to the Commission's approach may be the length of time it takes for progress to be felt.

SUCCESS MEASURES: County and Regional Perspectives

County and regional groups serving the Tug Hill area are somewhat positive about the Commission, with some specific reservations. Two main county-level groups are affected: the four legislatures or boards of supervisors and the three county planning agencies.

County governments have not hindered the Commission's activities or its search for state funds, but neither have they provided active support until recently. At first, all four counties adopted a neutral, wait-and-see attitude to the Commission's formation. This attitude has changed somewhat, but slowly. On the one hand, those county officials interviewed warmly supported Commission programs. In at least Lewis County, the county government is represented directly on the Commission. But several also voiced suspicion of the Commission creating programs and then disbanding, leaving the county to pick up an unaffordable tab for new services in rural areas.

This reluctance is illustrated by Lewis County's 1978 approval and then refusal of a Commission-sponsored IPA grant for a pilot office of town and village assistance.[16] The county rejected the grant upon learning that the money was not guaranteed past one year. Various Oneida and Jefferson county agencies reacted similarly, until Oneida County Cooperative Extension agreed to sponsor the program.

Until recently, relations between the Tug Hill Commission and county planning boards were also weak. This is also true of regional planning agencies: the Black River-St. Lawrence, Herkimer-Oneida, and Central New York regional planning boards. Concentrating on town-level planning, the Commission did not focus until recenty on coordination with either of these groups. In addition, these organizations tend to have an urban orientation; rural Tug Hill is somewhat peripheral to their concerns.

Three Tug Hill counties have both county planning boards and county planning departments with professional county planners; Lewis County has only a county planning board comprised of county legislators. The Lewis County Planning Board has no strong objections to Commission planning activities in the eleven Lewis County towns; but then, it cannot provide these services on its own.

In the three county planning departments, a similar reservation was voiced with varying degrees of concern: that Commission staff are duplicating county services and creating a demand for planning assistance that the county cannot fill. One county planner termed it "drumming up business without any clear way of getting things done." In addition, all de-emphasized Tug Hill as a viable region. They also wondered if some cooperative groupings are artificial, and expressed reservations whether cooperative groups are appropriate for any but the most rural, isolated core area towns.

Oswego County planner works on sketch with members of North Shore Cooperative Planning Board.

The Commission's local planning services could have been undertaken by county staff. But in numerous cases, towns turning to the Commission had previously been unsuccessful in obtaining these services from their county. Counties must often allocate services by population, land area, and political pull; this often leaves small rural Tug Hill towns last in line. A 1972 study of the Herkimer-Oneida Comprehensive Planning Program noted extensive comprehensive planning activity, but little evidence of use of this information for implementation, particularly in rural areas.[17] The Commission's generation of need for planning services may, in some ways, serve as a nuisance value, in pushing counties to fill needs they previously neglected.

All three regional planning agencies provide some local planning assistance but focus much of their attention elsewhere. The Black River-St. Lawrence Regional Planning Board formed in 1972 by four counties, including Jefferson and Lewis, began with region-wide studies and now answers county and local government re-quests, but does not provide any organizational aid. The Central New York Regional Planning and Development Board has a strong urban orientation, because most of its region's population is urban and because of its federal funding requirements. While these agen-cies do not appear overly concerned about duplication, one regional planner remarked, "Nothing is worse than two planners going into one town." And a serious question remains as to whether the Tug Hill Commission adds more to the confusion of local, regional, and state agencies serving the Tug Hill areas than it counteracts through a strong local assistance program.

The Commission has recently tried to improve coordination with the area's county and regional agencies. For example, staff is cur-rently shared with the Black River-St. Lawrence Regional Planning Board, the Herkimer-Oneida Comprehensive Planning Program, and the Oswego County Planning Department. In 1978, a joint resolution of planning purposes was signed with the Black River-St. Lawrence Regional Planning Board and the Jefferson County Planning Department.[18] And in January 1980, the commissioners passed a resolution commending area agencies for their cooperation.

SUCCESS MEASURES: State government and Outside Concerns

Clearly, the Tug Hill Commission has had a substantial impact at the local level, and relations with county and regional agencies seem to be improving. But what about state-level and outside concerns and expectations? How has the Commission fulfilled state-level ob-jectives that were a partial reason for its creation? How has it bal-anced state and local interests? How has it managed potential goal conflicts amount all these groups? And how has it satisfied state-level accountability?

The Commission has convinced most state-level groups that its programs are of some use to the state. But the Commission's creation was not a result of strong state-level or outside interest in the Tug

Hill area, and this situation has not changed dramatically. Local actions have, so far, not substantially challenged these relatively weak outside concerns.

Various state-level and outside groups have, however, expressed concern for the Tug Hill area at one time or another. These include: the state legislature and staff, both as individuals and as a group; individual state agencies, in particular DEC; outside recreational interests, such as the Adirondack Mountain Club and county sportsmen's federations; environmental groups such as the Environmental Planning Lobby and Sierra Club; the increasing number of absentee landowners in the Tug Hill area; and corporate interests, especially Georgia Pacific Corporation.

In the minds of many state legislators, the Tug Hill Commission is still a nonissue. Yet state-level support for the Commission's rural resource management approach is growing as individuals become more familiar with its work. The area's assembly members have indicated their support of the Commission, and Senator Barclay remains a strong proponent. The Commission is increasingly supported by state legislators with concerns for environmental conservation and local government, and by many Democrats as well as upstate Republicans. There is also a recently awakened, though not powerful, interest among legislative and state agency staff regarding the Commission's approach as a potential model for rural regional planning. And statewide environmental groups, while officially neutral, are leaning toward a positive view of the Commission's work.

On the other hand, the Commission's future is far from assured. Some individuals at the state level or members of outside groups see the Commission's efforts as insufficient to represent outside interests, and raise a few basic criticisms. They argue that local government controls alone may not provide adequate protection for the Tug Hill area's natural resource base, particularly in the case of another massive development proposal. Some state agencies expected to see emergence of regional authority and more scheduled progress toward land use controls; thus, another criticism is that the Commission appears to be "doing nothing," and serves only as a funnel for state money into the area. One state official thought the Commission "leaned over so far backward to appear to be on the side of the locals that it abdicated its responsibility as a state agency, and, as such, to support other state agencies." Some fear that cooperative planning boards may fall apart when the Commission disbands.

Instead of incorporating state concerns in local land use decisions through some form of state regulation, mandated planning, or creation of a regional authority, the Tug Hill Commission adopted a different approach. By prompting local governments to plan, it has exerted influence on local land use decisions and encouraged a balance of local and state values concerning the Tug Hill area. And by increasing local government effectiveness and encouraging local adoption of state-level land use laws, it has responded to many outside land use management concerns. The Commission has not forced its views on local governments through regulation, but has presented them through planning assistance, education, and the structuring of land use issues in terms understandable by local government officials and citizens.

At least in the Tug Hill area, this approach appears effective. The core area towns are perhaps the best example. Most local land use controls so far adopted reflect local awareness of natural resource and development issues that extend beyond individual town boundaries. Increased local capabilities for managing their own affairs also promote the state's interests and respond to outside concerns.

This attempt to incorporate outside interests through influence rather than regulation has had several effects. First, numerous local governments with previously negative attitudes to planning and zoning are now making land use decisions. Second, through cooperative planning, individual towns have a forum and incentive to consider at least a multitown perspective on the environment and to produce work of higher quality. Third, local governments are encouraged to think beyond their towns' immediate self-interest. Finally, the Commission's higher level support for local decision-making can help town or village officials incorporate outside values and make politically unpopular decisions.

How well do the local land use controls so far instituted protect the entire natural resource base of the Tug Hill area? The Commission has endeavored to set up a system to handle development pressures at the local level through cooperative planning boards, but this system has no regionwide provisions for reviewing developments

Photograph courtesy of David M. Doody.

with regional impact, no regionwide regulations, and no formal regionwide plan.

When the Commission was formed, future development and its impacts on the area were expected to be severe. In 1976 the Commission summarized these predictions as follows: "Over the next twenty years, in the absence of corrective measures, most Tug Hill core lands will be owned by nonresidents. Vacation homes will multiply . . . . Property taxes will rise, and many Tug Hill citizens will no longer be able to afford to stay. . . . Forests and farms will wither, taking with them wood and food processing industries. The watershed will then be threatened."[19] These dire predictions may have been somewhat overdrawn. Nonetheless, development pressure in the Tug Hill has been less immediate, more fragmented and incremental than in such areas as the Adirondacks.

Although the cooperative system has not yet been fully established or tested by any large-scale development proposal, it may be adequate to handle the development pressures expected. The cooperative board system potentially allows for formal consideration of development impacts on more than one municipality, and also provides a mechanism for influencing decisions made through existing state authority, such as DEC water and sewer permits. It seems best able to handle smaller-scale, fragmented development, rather than massive development proposals.

A formal regionwide permit system or land use management plan may not be appropriate for this region. First, there is at present no regionwide environmental or other interest group that could monitor a permanent agency with regional regulatory powers to maintain a proper balance between environmental and development interests. Second, a sense of the Tug Hill region as a whole is weak, socially and economically. A regional effort might face more trouble from lack of cooperation than it could compensate for by regionwide coordination. Third, regional regulation is only necessary when there are dominant regionwide resource concerns that are not adequately protected through existing local or state institutions. In the Tug Hill area, this does not appear to be the case. If a regionwide challenge arises in the future, Tug Hill communities may find their experience with the Commission useful. And fourth, because of strong local attitudes toward home rule, local governments in this area may actually perform better if they are not forced into planning and tied to a timetable.

One potential weakness is the voluntary nature of the cooperative land use regulation system. Not all towns have chosen to become involved, and those involved in planning activities may not choose to adopt regulatory controls. But there are several motives for nonparticipation. Some towns have already developed land use controls on their own; others have been motivated to individual action by the example of their neighbors in cooperative boards; only a few towns have no land use controls at all. And perhaps more important, from an outside interest perspective, 245,000 acres of the most environmentally critical portion of this area, the central Tug Hill upland or core area, are protected by regulations of seven towns in the CTHPB.

In summary, the Tug Hill Commission has not been a "do-nothing" agency, but rather one that has done things differently. Instead of regional planning and regulation, the Commission has focused on improving local governments' total management capability. The beginnings of regional cooperation are provided. More centralized controls can be developed if they are needed at some future date.

While not all state and outside groups are completely satisfied, the Commission has incorporated most major outside concerns in some fashion. Nevertheless, it has concentrated on satisfying local concerns, occasionally at the expense of a particular state agency or program. But this is perhaps the only politically feasible way to work with local governments in this area. To force planning, land use regulations, or regional cooperation among Tug Hill towns might very well have resulted in the Commission's demise.

LONG-TERM PROSPECTS FOR TUG HILL PROGRAMS

The Tug Hill Commission, by law a temporary state commission, has resolved to disband by March 31, 1981. Long-term prospects for the survival of Commission programs cannot be completely assessed at this point. Many essential decisions regarding what form long-term support may take are not yet made.

As part of its phase-out program, the Commission attempted to develop an orderly policy for transition of the critical parts of its programs to local agencies. This had developed into a significant effort, involving so far two advisory groups of local leaders, two public forums, and a stepped-up emphasis on relationships with regional and county agencies that might assume responsibility for parts of its programs.

Nevertheless, long-term survival of accomplishments is a crucial question. Of primary importance is whether the cooperative planning boards have developed a local planning competency independent of the Commission or will require continuing support. Can these boards successfully function without some form of long-term technical or financial assistance? If not, which higher-level institutions can best provide this aid?

Other Commission functions, such as citizen education programs and research on areawide issues, must also be evaluated for their long-term need. What are the major issues for the Tug Hill area? Do Commission programs do anything about them? Should the programs be continued? And, if so, who should provide them?

The cooperative planning process developed as one response to existing local governments' handling of outside development pressures. Higher-level assistance has substantially improved this capacity. Yet many of the factors that led to cooperative planning are still present.

Most local governments in the Tug Hill area still may not possess the financial, technical, and organizational resources to operate these cooperative planning boards entirely on their own. Planning is a continuous process, requiring constant updating of previous work. This is especially true of implementation, as local planning boards continue to review development proposals. In particular, the core town members of the Cooperative Tug Hill Planning Board are vulnerable, as they are the poorest towns in the four-county Tug Hill area and are also the most critical in terms of natural resource protection.

Besides assistance to cooperative and local planning boards, the Commission has provided a wide range of technical assistance to local government officials. This assistance has built independence and strengthened local capabilities. But some of it is day-to-day advice, roughly equivalent to that provided by consultants or lawyers on retainer for more wealthy suburban towns. Small rural communities do not have the financial capability to purchase these services, sometimes not even on a joint basis with neighboring towns which may be as poor as they are. Yet some suggest that although the priority placed on these services in these towns is high enough to request outside assistance, it is not critical enough in the priorities of townspeople to divert scarce local resources to it when they are forced to make such decisions.

The need for local assistance and the inability of local governments to afford it was stressed by participants in the November 1979 workshops on the Commission's future, and by those involved in cooperative and local planning.[20] One North Shore town board member commented, "The program's supposed to get towns on their own feet, but this just can't be done; we've got a long way to go yet." A SRCPB member commented, "Towns should put up the money, but

I don't see them doing it." In the JSCB area, another comment was heard: "When we stop getting Commission assistance, we'll still have an area which transcends local political authority. What do you do?" Further, towns in three cooperative planning board areas are already contributing funds to their cooperative boards.

At the workshops, many expressed the conviction that the state should provide financial assistance. A number voiced tentative support for some form of a continued regional commission. But this assistance need not come from a state-created regional commission, temporary or permanent. Such an authority has significant drawbacks. Some Commission critics are concerned about duplication of services; some needs of Tug Hill communities could be met through existing government. In addition, opposition to a permanent regional agency by area governments and citizens could be strong.

One possibility for delivering assistance to rural local governments is through county governments. The Commission's pilot local government assistance program through Oneida County Cooperative Extension is an attempt to develop a workable model. Other possible arrangements include involvement of regional planning boards, state line agencies such as DEC, or splitting Commission functions among several organizations.

The counties appear closest to the towns in everyday working relationships and would appear to be the most likely source of assistance. However, whether rural Tug Hill local governments have the political strength to implement this approach is uncertain. A major factor is that the Commission has worked with Tug Hill towns at the expense of developing strong relationships with the four counties. As one county official phrased it, "If the Commission continues in any form, relationships with the counties must be defined." Furthermore, assuming Commission functions entail risks for any organization, including the county. Some county officials also feel they are being stuck with paying for state programs they never asked for. All four counties are at present severely limited financially, and are unable or unwilling to embark on new major programs. An illustration of this financial situation is the Oswego County Legislature's recent requirement of a charge to all municipalities receiving county planning assistance. At the same time, many county officials tend to agree with a statement at the 1979 workshops: "If you want control, you must pay for it."

The Commission's role as areawide spokesman is exercised through lobbying at the state level, visibility of the Commission as an areawide organization, travels of Commission staff outside the area, and citizen education programs within the area to raise awareness of broader issues. No attempt will be made here to assess the long-term importance of this function. But this largely unrecognized Commission role would no longer be filled in the Commission's absence. It is conceivable, but probably unlikely, that the counties or cooperative planning boards could support such activities. The principal barrier is likely to be lack of recognition of adequate self-interest in regionwide issues affecting Tug Hill, a situation the Commission was forced to adapt to in its own programs.

6 Lessons for Other Rural Areas

THE TUG HILL APPROACH: How It Differs

Rural local governments are often beset with a variety of problems and limitations, many not of their own making, that reduce their capability to effectively manage the use of rural resources.

Many conventional approaches to resolving these problems, usually of urban origin, do not appear to work well in rural areas. Often professional planners' attitudes and philosophies differ from those of the residents. The kinds and amounts of services provided are often inadequate. The degree of local involvement in higher-level decisions and the creation of often somewhat artificial regions also contribute to limitations of conventional approaches. Thus innovative techniques are needed for dealing with rural land use issues.

The Tug Hill Commission has developed its own approach to meeting these problems by combining several methods to strengthen rural local government capabilities, improve local resource management, incorporate state concerns, and balance state and local needs. Cooperative multitown planning has emerged out of this process as an unusual variation on standard regional planning methods. But the Commission also serves as a regional study group, a community development agency, a local assistance service, an area spokesman, and an educator of local citizens.

This unusual combination of methods from several conventional approaches presents a model of diversity and flexibility in dealing with rural local governments. As such, it presents an alternative to conventional approaches for treating the problems of rural areas.

139

How does this approach differ from the methods often used by regional planning agencies? One difference is the degree of emphasis on the process of cooperation among, and with, local governments. Formal cooperative planning among rural local governments is highly unusual; cooperative enforcement is unique.

As to technical assitance, many planners have provided similar services for years. But the flexibility, the manner of delivery, the outreach, and the translation of the planning process into understandable terms are unusual aspects of the Tug Hill Commission's assistance program. Few outside state-level agencies coming into a rural area approach local involvement in this fashion. And the Commission's status as an independent state agency, with few artificial outside constraints imposed on its work, also distinguishes it.

This is not a regional approach in the conventional sense. It does not employ one standardized method. Nor does it set regionwide regulations and guidelines, or produce a formal, regional plan. It allows subregional differences within the area to emerge, even turning these to advantage in obtaining local support.

The approach works toward a rural policy by reliance on local decision-making and concentrates on preparing local governments to accept the responsibility for coping with regional forces often considered to be beyond local control. This reliance on local decision-making is consistent with a recent study accompanying the American Law Institute's Model Rural Development Code, which suggests that 90 percent of land use decisions can be handled locally.[1]

Furthermore, assistance with local land use regulations is only part of the Commission's program, which has grown into a broader-based effort that also emphasizes other ways of dealing with local resource management. Rural land use issues are the vehicle for a process of strengthening local government capabilities. The Commission has merged a community-organizing approach with conventional planning techniques and applied this to regional land use decision-making.

Support for this type of approach is growing. For example, the Council of State Planning Agencies has made several recommendations for a new rural land use and development strategy including increased free or low-cost local technical assistance delivered through an outreach program; a state-local sharing of costs to provide needed professionals to part-time rural governments; formation of cooperative areawide consortiums; and the encouraging of specific local actions within a broad areawide framework.[2] Recently, a major federal rural policy document identified a need for circuit riders and technical assistance programs to serve small communities.[3]

Even Robert Healy, a strong supporter of regional land use control, notes the possible limitations of relying exclusively on conventional regulatory mechanisms: "It is important to separate the failure of specific local controls from the shortcomings of the concept. . . . If local zoning has failed, the fault may lie with the tool rather than with the level of government that wields it."[4]

How well have the Commission's efforts worked? Results vary among the five cooperative planning areas, and its successes have some limitations. But some general successes can be recognized: the existence and functioning of local and joint planning boards in much of the Tug Hill area; improved land use regulations of many local governments; some increase in local government capability; a partial breach of traditional rural communication barriers; a small group of educated citizens well versed in land use issues and the workings of local government; and a somewhat greater awareness among area citizens about land use issues. The Commission has satisfied a variety of local interest groups, including some initially hostile local governments. At the same time, while its programs do not "save" Tug Hill for the state, they do incorporate most state and outside concerns.

WHAT MADE IT WORK?

What lessons can be learned from this process for application to other areas?

Several factors helped make it work in the Tug Hill area. These include the attitudes of staff and commissioners to the task at hand; provision of local assistance and training in many subjects; an unusual degree of agency flexibility, freedom, and loose time constraints, allowing a stage-by-stage approach; development of mutual acceptance of local and state priorities and approaches; and strong state legislative support.

ATTITUDES TO THE TASK AT HAND

One major factor in the Commission's success is the makeup of the original Commission and initial attitudes of both commissioners and staff to their task, the Tug Hill area, and its people. Commissioners represented a variety of area interests, from business to environmental, and all were residents of the Tug Hill counties. This contributed to reduced local hostility to the group and an increased understanding of the area involved.

Initial attitudes of the volunteer commissioners toward their job directly influenced the Commission's success. Besides being strongly committed to the Commission's charge and objectives, most did not have preconceived notions as to their role or recommendations. For example, the commissioners did not immediately assume the need for a regional regulatory approach. And most importantly, they were committed to involving local governments and citizens in decision-making, including local concerns in their recommendations, and assisting local governments in the area.

Attitudes of Commission staff, a highly visible component of day-to-day operations, were equally important in making this approach work. Staff members have been highly service oriented, both to the Commission and to area local governments. They have been sensitive to local concerns and dedicated to working with local government and allowing local decision-making. Planning has been approached as an educational process, with local government as its focus. Staff abilities in relating to people were another key factor in Commission effectiveness. For example, one CTHPB member admired the way staff went "door to door." "That personal contact is important," he said.

Initial Commission decisions, such as choice of a service-oriented executive director and holding public forums in the Tug Hill area, set the tone for later policy. These decisions were a direct result of initial Commission attitudes. In addition, the Commission was highly flexible in its early decisions and in revising policy recommendations in response to local concerns.

LOCAL ASSISTANCE: What, How, When

The assistance provided to local governments, and the manner in which this assistance was provided, were crucial to the success of the Commission's effort. Besides planning assistance, this included legal, financial, technical, and other local government aid. Community organizing assistance complemented planning aid to strengthen community abilities in land use management.

The manner and timing of assistance were important. One staff member noted, "We must build a bond with them first, before they will admit to having concerns." Before effective assistance can be delivered, towns must first realize they have problems. Next, individual help must be easily available. Finally comprehensive programs may bring communities together to help solve their own problems. Community organizing and outreach are necessary corollaries to working with local governments. But no technical assistance program can work if there is no recognition of a valid need. The Commission's cooperative planning experience demonstrates that a local crisis is an important stimulant to help generate or realize a need for assistance.

Some specific Commission activities deserve comment. For one, the rural aide played a significant role as a complement to the planner. Also, the few times that Commission staff anticipated local problems or opportunities and provided widespread assistance were highly productive for local communities. One example is the Commission's effort to help local governments pass local wetlands laws to meet a state deadline.

Individual problem solving in the technical assistance program, while helpful to a particular municipality, used much Commission staff time. But programs that delivered specific results, such as attracting grant money or solving a well-defined local problem, led several towns to undertake cooperative planning.

The Commission, in response to local reactions, altered the emphasis of its planning program. At first apparently not highly flexible, the staff lessened emphasis on natural resource planning along the CTHPB model and grew more open to other goals and concerns. This flexibility is crucial to an effective program.

Finally, technical assistance, not just to local planning boards, but also to local elected officials, can provide a means of strengthening relationships with local leaders. In this area the Commission has been less uniformly successful. One county planner described it this way, "The people here are like anywhere else. If they sit on a planning board, it becomes a part of them. But they're not on the town board. Town boards aren't sitting through the sessions; they're not convinced."

FLEXIBILITY AND TIME

The Commission has enjoyed an unusual degree of freedom and flexibility in its work, allowing it to translate its goals into acceptable local modes, and with available time to do so. This also helped make possible the pursuit of a stage-by-stage experimental approach to land use planning. Many regional agencies relying on different funding sources and political support do not have this flexibility.

Contributing to the Commission's flexibility was its status as a temporary state commission independent of any other state agency, combined with its broad-ranging legislative charge. Lack of explicit state-level pressures to perform a certain way, particularly to institute a regional authority, was another factor which allowed flexibility. Furthermore, unrestricted state dollars put no serious allocation or time constraints on the Commission's progress, except for meeting its legislative reporting deadlines. Thus the Commission did not have to produce immediate results.

This situation, however, had at least three drawbacks. Temporary status created potential annual funding difficulties. And the Commission's association by area local officials with the state as another state entity worked against it. Also, local officials may be somewhat reluctant to cooperate with a temporary agency, for fear of being forced to finance programs when it is discontinued.

Perception of an areawide crisis by a number of concerned influential individuals sparked the Commission's formation, stimulating public discussion about the area's future. But during much of the Commission's period of operation, this crisis or any other, along with associated tensions, was not strongly perceived. The arousal of general citizen concern for this area, however, combined with less immediate development pressures, was responsible for lower-key but continuing attention to Tug Hill resources, creating a less tense but supportive atmosphere that made it possible for the Commission to engage in the time-consuming cooperative method it chose.

Other factors indigenous to the Tug Hill area were also partly responsible for the Commission's freedom to design and implement programs. The Tug Hill area is still relatively unknown to downstate areas and somewhat isolated. This anonymity acted to protect the Commission from serious statewide criticism. In addition, the existence of the Adirondack Park Agency nearby offered a distraction for major outside preservation interests and a focus for statewide concern.

As a result of all these factors, the Commission was able to experiment with the cooperative planning method initially in only one portion of the Tug Hill area. The experimental status of the first cooperative planning board did not threaten other towns, as a massive regional effort might have. At the same time, the success of this innovation encouraged other communities to follow the example.

MUTUAL ACCEPTANCE OF PRIORITIES AND APPROACHES

A key aspect of the Commission's work, and one that distinguishes it from other similar agencies, is the degree to which local as well as state interests have been involved in policy making and implementation. In identifying issues, in determining ways of handling them, and in carrying out programs and recommendations, the Commission has managed to integrate local philosophies and outside concerns. As one observer phrased it, "The outside world cares about planning and zoning to protect the water and their skiing. They don't care about grants for snowplows. But to Tug Hill communities, planning is a vehicle for outside help."[5] By adopting a nonthreatening stance, involving local governments and citizens early in its work, and sweetening local acceptance with visible results, the Commission gradually built cooperation with many local governments in this potentially hostile area.

Emphasis on the role of local decision-making appears throughout the Commission's activities, from the first public forums within the area to present citizen education programs. When given adequate information and time to consider it, many Tug Hill local governments have supported some form of action for land use planning, environmental protection, and other issues of outside concern, provided they have the major say in these decisions. Yet the Commission did not force on local governments programs or actions suggested solely by outside concerns. For example, the Commission gradually substituted the subregional cooperative planning approach for its original recommendation of a regionwide land use control system.

Thus another key to the Commission's effectiveness was identifying priorities and developing programs that satisfied most outside and local concerns to at least some extent. In the Tug Hill area, this was largely accomplished through careful attention to the concerns of local governments and local interest groups.

STATE LEGISLATIVE SUPPORT

As a state-created and state-funded agency, the Commission required state legislative support to continue its activities and programs in the Tug Hill area. The single biggest element in this continued support has been the leadership of one influential state senator from the Tug Hill area. While this senator's support is not guaranteed each year, it has so far not failed to provide at least a large portion of the Commission requests. Because the Commission had this continuing state-level support, it could concentrate on area programs rather than on state policies, while enjoying the benefits of an independent commission status.

The Commission's strategy for political survival at the state level, consisting of a low profile and annual appropriations through the state budget process, helped prevent more forcefully expressed outside interest in, and opposition to, its programs. This, in turn, granted the agency more freedom to closely consider local as well as state and outside concerns.

The nature of state interests and concerns for the Tug Hill area also contributed to the Commission's effectiveness. Broad-based statewide interest was weakly expressed. Thus strong state pressures to produce immediate results or to push a particular solution were for the most part absent. Although this helped assure the Commission of some state support while not unduly restricting its activities, this also had disadvantages. Political survival is somewhat unpredictable.

Annual extensions in the budgeting process have potential for unexpected reductions, compared to special legislation granting a multi-year authority. This arrangement for state support is somewhat unusual and may not be repeatable elsewhere, either within New York State or outside it.

ADDITIONAL FACTORS SPECIFIC TO TUG HILL

Several factors specific to the Tug Hill area, in addition to those already mentioned, deserve further comment. These include the role of the Adirondack Park Agency (APA), the nature and size of the study area, the lack of strong regional identity, and the character and attitudes of local leaders.

Besides calling attention away from the Tug Hill Commission, the APA served as an example to residents of the Tug Hill area of the state's regulatory approach to regional resource protection, which was highly unpopular with many local residents of the Adirondacks. This factor was especially strong in Lewis and Oneida counties, both of which also have towns in the Adirondack Park. The Commission program appeared, in contrast, to be nonthreatening and locally oriented for Tug Hill officials. Much of the early hostility expressed toward the Tug Hill Commission was motivated by fears of regional regulation on the pattern of the APA.

The size of the Tug Hill study area also helped foster the Commission's success. The thirty-nine towns and villages are, in total area, smaller than many regional planning areas where direct local government assistance would be much more difficult to provide due to area size alone.

Furthermore, as previously noted, the Tug Hill area lacks a strong regional identity outside the sparsely inhabited core area. Both population and local political power are concentrated in the peripheral towns, with the core area acting as a communication barrier. This is partly responsible for weak local support for areawide consideration of issues, leading to the adoption of the Commission's subregional, locally oriented approach.

Finally, the influence of the character and attitudes of local leaders is illustrated by the substantial role of motivated and concerned core area town officials in initiating the first cooperative planning board. Perhaps paradoxically, these officials were motivated in part by perceived threats of state intervention, as well as massive change through development.

LESSONS FOR OTHER RURAL AREAS

The Tug Hill Commission has publicized its cooperative approach to strengthening rural local government as "an experiment to develop a model for rural land use planning." While the methods developed so far are not entirely unique, nor appropriate to all rural situations, the Commission's approach appears to be a feasible alternative for strengthening local government capability, developing means for the management of rural resources, including land use, and enlarging the base of considerations that go into local decisions. It can be especially useful for areas defined on the basis of a unifying natural characteristic that require intergovernmental cooperation where no such mechanism presently exists. It also has potential for reducing local hostility to higher-level, particularly state, involvement in local land use management. Additional benefits may include improved communication among local governments, and between local and state government, on a variety of issues besides land use.

One should begin with the understanding that reliance on local decision-making is the essence of this approach, coupled with an extensive effort to bolster that decision-making through broadly based local assistance. The key principles of this method are flexibility and diversity. A multiple approach, employing elements of several disciplines, can be more acceptable to different local groups, regardless of their goals, than a narrowly defined or single issue approach. Flexibility, in terms of attitudes, definition of issues, programs, and approach is necessary.

A condensation of some of the principal elements of this approach, and the lessons that may be drawn from them, follow, for possible application in other areas.

ASSESSING THE RURAL AREA INVOLVED

1. The prospective rural area to be served must be carefully examined, to determine the degree to which it coheres as one region

or several. Planning and other programs must take this into account. If one regionwide approach is not feasible, perhaps fostering several subregional identities can help.

2. Distinguishing geographic, social, or economic characteristics specific to a particular area, such as natural boundaries, traditional social territorial identifications, and local economic patterns, are often critical considerations in developing potentially effective approaches.

3. Some strong regional or subregional relationship must exist to bring communities together, such as a common natural resource base or similar land use problems. In addition, the presence of an obvious area crisis is one of the most effective motivators of local action.

BALANCING OUTSIDE AND LOCAL INTERESTS

1. Tradeoffs between outside and local objectives must be expected. Success of these tradeoffs depends largely on staff freedom and flexibility to develop programs that mesh diverse viewpoints. To do this requires expertise, funding, and an open attitude.

2. While some accommodation of outside interests is possible in this approach, it is not certain if strongly divergent and forcefully expressed state and local objectives can be compromised in this manner. The depth and magnitude of outside interests, and the degree to which they mesh with local concerns, should be assessed before the start of any program.

3. Representatives of the agency's board of directors should be selected from the area involved, should represent all major diverse interest groups within and outside the area, and should have solid reputations within the area in addition to their higher-level connections. Otherwise the agency will suffer from lack of credibility before it begins.

4. Emphasis should not be on trying to change local attitudes, but instead building upon them and seeking compromise.

RESPECTING THE SPECIAL NATURE OF RURAL AREAS

1. Planners and other staff members must develop a sensitivity to local perceptions, traditions, and motivations, even when ap-

parently different from their own. Staff should be carefully selected, with attention to their attitudes and experience in working with local government as well as their professional expertise. Maintaining an open-minded attitude and a faith in local decision-making, particularly with regard to planning goals, requires self-examination.

2. Along with conventional planning techniques, planners should utilize techniques based on principles of community organizing and community education. Planning can be most effective when practiced as an educational strategy, combined with local assistance for the organizational aspects of planning.

3. Technical assistance to local government officials is a crucial part of developing local government capabilities. Direct involvement of local elected officials improves the chances for success of local planning programs.

4. Planning programs are most effective when tied to individualized technical assistance. Visible results provide local motivation for engaging in a longer-term process with less immediate benefits. Technical assistance other than planning may prove to be what some communities need most.

5. Planners and other involved professionals should stand back to let local attitudes emerge and take advantage of local energies. But without a local crisis or a valid need to motivate a community, much staff energy can be wasted on trying to generate interest in its programs.

ALLOWING SUFFICIENT TIME TO MAKE THE PROCESS WORK

1. Working with rural local governments is a time-consuming process. Commitment and financial support that is assured for several years will bring best results. Programs with tight time schedules run the risk of being counterproductive if planners attempt to force actions on issues.

2. Staff requirements for this interactive approach are high. Overcommitment of limited staff resources is possible, especially if staff interest and dedication is strong. It may be wiser to serve a smaller number of municipalities well.

3. Some long-term continuing support must be provided for cooperative planning boards and other rural local government needs.

This should include organizational and educational support and training for local elected officials, as well as technical and planning assistance.

MAINTAINING RELATIONSHIPS WITH OTHER AGENCIES

1. Building links to existing agencies at the next highest level of local government (in New York, counties) can provide valuable support for agency activities and programs.

2. Careful attention must also be paid to the realities of higher level politics that support the agency, and to details of the funding process by which it survives. This is true for both state and federally supported agencies. Sufficient progress must be demonstrated in meeting higher-level objectives to reduce opposition at this level.

POSSIBLE ADAPTATIONS FOR BROADER APPLICATION

Without modification, the Tug Hill method will likely be less successful in at least three situations. First, in areas where development pressures are large scale or immediate, more rapid action may be required to protect the resource base. Secondly, where state concerns or those of statewide public interest groups are more forcefully expressed and play a major role in agency formation, more formal accounting of these concerns may be necessary. And thirdly, agreement on goals and methods may be more difficult in areas where state concerns differ markedly from those of area residents and governments, or where strong divergent interests within the region exist.

Where some of these conditions are present, the Tug Hill Commission's approach can be modified to fit particular situations. For example, certain elements alone can be used. Possible modifications include membership of a state or statewide representative on the agency or formal incorporation of diverse interest groups as more active partners in both the local planning process and in decisions. It can also be combined with some aspects of a regulatory approach to meet more immediate development pressures. Another possible ap-

St. Patrick's Church, Highmarket, recently renovated by descendants of early Tug Hill settlers. *Photograph courtesy of David M. Doody.*

plication is use of the cooperative method with groups of local elected officials in subregional councils. And in areas with a stronger regional identity and more uniform population distribution, cooperative boards could combine to form a regional board.

Notes

1—IN QUEST OF WORKABLE RURAL PLANNING AND DEVELOPMENT OPTIONS

1. Frank O. Sargent, *Rural Water Planning* (Montpelier, Vt.: privately published, 1979), p. 178. A textbook definition of "rural" that will hold up for all uses is difficult at best. "Rural" is a word indicating quality of life or setting as compared to "urban." *Webster's New Collegiate Dictionary* defines rural: "of or relating to country, country people or life, or agriculture." The U.S. Census defines an "urban" city or town as one having a population of 2,500 or more. Are the rest of the municipalities "rural" by default? No, this can only be a definition of population size and not of quality of surroundings. The federal government's use of "Standard Metropolitan Statistical Area" provides no clearer picture of what is urban or rural; many rural-like areas lie within SMSAs. Some additional references on what is "rural" are: Glenn V. Fuguitt, Paul R. Voss, and J. C. Doherty, *Growth and Change in Rural America*, Management & Control of Growth Series (Washington, D.C.: The Urban Land Institute, 1979), pp. 53–54; Thomas R. Ford, *Rural U.S.A., Persistence and Change* (Ames, Iowa: Iowa State University Press, 1978), pp. 3–9; and John Fraser Hart, *The Look of the Land* (Englewood Cliffs, N.J.: Prentice-Hall, 1975), pp. 169–70.

2. U.S. Advisory Commission on Intergovernmental Relations, *Urban and Rural America: Policies for Future Growth* (Washington, D.C.: ACIR, 1968), p. 59.

3. See, for discussion: Arthur J. Vidich and Joseph Bensman, *Small Town in Mass Society* (Princeton, N.J.: Princeton University Press, 1968); and Bert E. Swanson et al., *Small Towns and Small Towners,* vol. 79 (Beverly Hills, Calif.: Sage Library of Social Research, 1979).

4. Richard Babcock, *The Zoning Game* (Madison, Wis.: University of Wisconsin Press, 1966), pp. 153–54.

5. U.S. Advisory Commission on Intergovernmental Relations, *Substate Regionalism and the Federal System,* 6 vols. (Washington, D.C.: ACIR, 1974), 1:8.

6. See, for discussion: Robert G. Healy, *Land Use and the States* (Washington, D.C.: Resources for the Future, 1976); and Council of State Governments, *State Growth Management* (Lexington, Ky.: May 1976).

7. See, for example: Helen Ingram, "The Political Viability of Regional Water Institutions" (Tucson, Ariz.: University of Arizona Institute of Governmental Services, 1975).

8. Council of State Planning Agencies, *State Development Strategies for Rural Communities,* State Planning Series, no. 6 (1977), p. 13.

9. For a discussion of substate regionalism, see: U.S. Advisory Commission on Intergovernmental Relations, *Substate Regionalism,* 6 vols.; and *Regionalism Revisited* (Washington, D.C.: ACIR, June 1977).

10. For a discussion of federal rural economic development alternatives, see Council of State Planning Agencies, *State Development Strategies.*

11. J. Friedmann and C. Weaver, *Territory and Function: The Evolution of Regional Planning* (Berkeley, Calif.: University of California Press, 1979), p. 6.

12. See Philip Selznick, *TVA and the Grassroots: A Study in the Sociology of Formal Organization* (Berkeley, Calif.: University of California Press, 1949).

13. The Appalachian Regional Commission is described in Donald R. Rothblatt, *Regional Planning: The Appalachian Experience* (Lexington, Mass.: Lexington Books, 1971).

14. William R. Lassey, *Planning in Rural Environments* (New York: McGraw-Hill, 1977), p. 2.

15. Professor Howard Conklin, Department of Agricultural Economics, Cornell University, personal communications, December 1979.

16. Ian McHarg, *Design with Nature* (New York: Doubleday, 1969).

17. See F. O. Sargent, *Rural Environmental Planning* (Montpelier, Vt.: privately published, 1976).

18. In 1974 the U.S. Department of Housing and Urban Development produced regulations requiring "701" funds recipients to file land use plans for continued funds, as well as housing and other elements. This requirement forced agencies to specifically attend to land use as one element of their planning program.

19. Council of State Planning Agencies, *State Development Strategies*; and Council of State Governments, *State Growth Management.*

20. An introduction to the Hawaiian program can be found in Phyllis Myers, *Zoning Hawaii,* Conservation Foundation Special Report (April 1976), an analysis of the passage and implementation of Hawaii's land classification law.

21. See L. S. McKinsey, *A State Mandates Local Government Review: Montana,* University of California Studies on Policy and Change, no. 5 (Davis, Calif.: Institute of Governmental Affairs, January 1979). For Massachusetts, see: Massachusetts Growth Policy Project, *Cities and Town Centers: A Program for Growth* (Cambridge, Mass.: Massachusetts Institute of Technology, 1977); and Richard High, "Mixed Reviews for the Massachusetts Growth Policy," *Planning* (August 1979), pp. 24–27. The Washington effort is described in Council of State Governments, *State Growth Management,* pp. 76–83.

22. See: American Law Institute, *A Model Land Development Code* (Washington, D.C., 1977); and Luther Carter, *The Florida Experience: Land and Water Policy*

in a Growth State, Resources for the Future (Baltimore, Md.: Johns Hopkins Press, 1975).

23. The Florida criteria for defining critical natural areas were overturned by a state supreme court in November 1978 and subsequently revised by the legislature. For a discussion of critical area controls, see Daniel Mandelker, "Critical Area Controls," *Journal of American Institute of Planners* (January 1975). The Adirondack Park Agency is discussed in Chapter 2. For an early discussion of the Tahoe Regional Planning Agency, see Laurence D. Baxter, "Regional Politics and the Challenge of Environmental Planning," Environmental Quality Series, no. 22 (Davis, Calif.: University of California Institute of Governmental Affairs, December 1974). An overview of the current situation is provided in Donald Saint-Just, "High Stakes at Lake Tahoe," *Environmental Comment* (February 1980), p. 9.

24. For a discussion of California's coastal program, see: Melvin Mogulof, *Saving the Coast: California's Experiment in Land Use Control* (Lexington, Mass.: Lexington Books, 1975); Stanley S. Scott, *Governing California's Coast* (Berkeley, Calif.: University of California Institute of Governmental Studies, 1975); or Robert G. Healy, *Protecting the Golden Shore* (Washington, D.C.: The Conservation Foundation, 1978).

25. An early account of Vermont's experience is Phyllis Myers, *So Goes Vermont* (Washington, D.C.: The Conservation Foundation, 1974). See also Schuyler Jackson, "Report of the Environmental Board to the Governor on the Administration of Act 250" (Montpelier, Vt.: 1976); and J. Jackson Walter, "The Law of the Land: Development Legislation in Maine and Vermont," *Maine Law Review* 23 (1973): 315, for an overview of both programs. Vermont's program is also reviewed in Michael Kintner, *In Pursuit of a Rational Land Use Policy: Vermont and New York Experiment in State Planning and Control* (Master's thesis, Cornell University, 1977).

26. Bert Swanson, *Small Towns and Small Towners,* p. 13; and "Small Town Revitalization Case Studies," *Journal of American Institute of Planners* (January 1977).

27. New York State's wide range of experience in land use planning is discussed in Chapter 2 in the section "The State: Politics and Attitudes."

28. See, for example: Anthony J. Catanese, *Planners and Local Politics: Impossible Dreams* (London: Sage Press, 1974); Alan J. Hahn, "Planning in Rural Areas," *Journal of the American Institute of Planners* (1970); and William R. Lassey, *Planning in Rural Environments,* who wrote: "Rural planning may require a radically different conception and approach" from urban planning (p. 8).

29. Based on interviews with local officials. See also Temporary State Commission on Tug Hill, *Preparing for the Future* (Watertown, N.Y.: March 1976), pp. 11, 16. It should be noted that disagreement exists over this statement. Some felt the Tug Hill area's preservation to be critical; others saw Tug Hill as of no statewide importance.

2—THE TUG HILL COMMISSION: Its Context

1. State University of New York (SUNY), College of Environmental Science and Forestry, *Resources of the Tug Hill Region* (Syracuse, N.Y.: February 1974).

2. Sandy Marvinney, "Tug Hill: A Profile of the Region," *New York State Conservationist* (August–September 1975), p. 1.

3. Harold E. Samson, *Tug Hill Country* (North Country Books: 1971), pp. i–ii.

4. SUNY, *Resources of the Tug Hill Region*.

5. Ibid., pp. 11–12; and Temporary State Commission on Tug Hill, *Preparing for the Future* (Watertown, N.Y.: February 1976), p. 9.

6. SUNY, *Resources of the Tug Hill Region*, p. 92. 1976–77 total was officially recorded at the Hooker measuring station for the U.S. National Oceanic and Atmospheric Administration.

7. Ibid., p. 8.

8. Institute of Man and Science, *The Communities of the Tug Hill Region* (Rensselaerville, N.Y.: 1974), p. 13.

9. SUNY, *Resources of the Tug Hill Region*, pp. 321–24.

10. Lyle S. Raymond, Jr., "Tug Hill: Defining a Meaningful Area for Regional Development," *Proceedings of the Northern New York-Lake Champlain Environmental Conference* (Chazy, N.Y.: Institute for Man and His Environment, 1974).

11. Temporary State Commission on Tug Hill, *Preliminary Findings* (Watertown, N.Y.: March 1975), p. 67.

12. Population projections from: Oswego County Planning Department; Oneida County Planning Department; Cooperative Tug Hill Planning Board, *Tug Hill Resource Management Plan* (Watertown, N.Y.: 1976), p. 20; and SUNY, *Resources of the Tug Hill Region*.

13. For information on the area's economy, see: J. David Bowman and Laurence E. Goss, *Economic Studies of the Tug Hill Region* (Watertown, N.Y.: Temporary State Commission on Tug Hill, December 1974); and Temporary State Commission, *Preliminary Findings*.

14. SUNY, *Resources of the Tug Hill Region*, p. 144.

15. For information on the area's agriculture, see: Bowman, *Economic Studies*, SUNY, *Resources of the Tug Hill Region*; and Margaret Parsons and James Murray, *The Use, Value, and Taxation of Tug Hill Lands* (Watertown, N.Y.: Temporary State Commission on Tug Hill, September 1974).

16. For information on land use trends, see: Parsons, *Use, Value, and Taxation*; James Barwick, *Property Taxes in Tug Hill* (Watertown, N.Y.: Temporary State Commission on Tug Hill, June 1976); and Temporary State Commission, *Land Taxes in Tug Hill* (draft, 1980).

17. This section on resident attitudes is based on: interviews conducted with area residents and local officials; Institute of Man and Science, *Communities*; Benjamin Coe et al., *Citizen Participation in Tug Hill Studies* (Watertown, N.Y.: Temporary State Commission on Tug Hill, March 1975) (transcripts of 1974 public forums); and

Donald Exford et al., *Public Comments on the Tug Hill Commission's Preliminary Findings* (Watertown, N.Y.: Temporary State Commission on Tug Hill, October 1975).

18. Institute of Man and Science, *Communities*, p. 10.

19. Watertown *Times*, April 8, 1975. Montague, in Lewis County, has the lowest population (58 in 1970) of any town in the state. With the Commission's aid, Montague subsequently unscrambled its finances.

20. Institute of Man and Science, *Communities*, p. 32.

21. SUNY, *Resources of the Tug Hill Region*, pp. 314–16; and Benjamin Coe et al., *Land Use Policy Development in the Rural Tug Hill Area of New York State* (Watertown, N.Y.: Temporary State Commission on Tug Hill, 1976), 3:36–38.

22. Georgia Pacific leases much of its land to sportsmen's clubs as one method of deriving income for property taxes.

23. Parsons, *Use, Value, and Taxation*, pp. 24–25, Appendix A; and Barwick, *Property Taxes*, p. 3.

24. The development proposal referred to is that of Horizon Corporation in 1971, on some 63,000 acres. An earlier development, Indian Hills, was proposed for the town of Redfield in the 1960s.

25. See: Temporary State Commission, *Preliminary Findings*, pp. 81–85; Parsons, *Use, Value, and Taxation*, Appendix B; and Institute for Man and His Environment, *A Recreation Study and Plan for Tug Hill* (Watertown, N.Y.: Temporary State Commission on Tug Hill, 1974).

26. New York State's wide range of experience in land use planning is discussed in Chapter 2 in the section "The State: Politics and Attitudes."

27. Temporary State Commission, *Preparing for the Future*, p. 32. The Tug Hill area was identified as a critical headwaters area by the state as early as a 1926 state planning report.

28. Temporary State Commission, *Preliminary Findings*, p. 28; and Cooperative Tug Hill Planning Board, *Resource Management*, p. 31.

29. Section 1, Article XIV, New York State Constitution states, "Forest Preserve as now fixed by law, shall be forever kept as wild forest lands." In addition to all state forest lands within the Adirondack Park boundary (popularly called the "blue line"), this applies to a small number of Tug Hill parcels which, though outside the boundary of the park, are in Lewis or Oneida counties—designated forest preserve counties since they lie, in part, within the park's boundary.

30. New York State Commission of Housing and Regional Planning, *New York State Planning Report* (May 7, 1926).

31. For further information on New York's history of state planning, see: Michael Heiman, *An Evaluation of State Land Use Planning and Development Control in the Adirondacks* (Master's thesis, Cornell University, 1975), p. 225; U.S. Advisory Commission on Intergovernmental Relations, *Substate Regionalism and the Federal System*, 6 vols. (Washington, D.C.: ACIR, 1974), 2; "Regional Governance: Promise and Performance" (Washington, D.C.: ACIR, 1974), pp. 270–82 on New York State; Michael R. Kintner, *In Pursuit of a Rational Land Use Policy* (Master's

thesis, Cornell University 1977); and Howard Conklin, *Rural Land Use Planning in the Northeast* (Ithaca, N.Y.: Cornell University, unpublished draft, 1980).

32. New York State Senate Bill S.9028 (1970).

33. Three regional planning and development boards in New York State serve primarily rural areas: Black River-St. Lawrence, Lake Champlain-Lake George, and Southern Tier West regional planning and development boards. The Tug Hill study area lies within the bounds of: Black River-St. Lawrence, Central New York, and Herkimer-Oneida Comprehensive regional planning boards.

34. More detailed information on these state laws can be found in William G. Lesher, "Land Use Laws in New York State" (Ithaca, N.Y.: Cornell University, Department of Agricultural Economics, December 1975). This legislation includes: Wild, Scenic and Recreational Rivers, 1972; Tidal Wetlands, 1973; Floodplain Protection, 1974; State Environmental Quality Review, 1975; and Freshwater Wetlands Quality Review, 1975.

35. Local conservation commissions can be created as branches of local government under state enabling legislation passed in 1970 (section 239-x, article 12-F, General Muncipal Law). County-level environmental management councils may also be formed (section 0101-0115, article 47, Conservation Law).

36. Recommendations of the Temporary Study Commission on the Future of the Adirondacks are detailed in *The Future of the Adirondack Park* (Albany, N.Y.: 1970). See also, for description of the plan and agency operation: Michael Heiman, *An Evaluation of State Land Use Planning and Development Control in the Adirondacks* (Master's thesis, Cornell University, 1975); Michael Kintner, *In Pursuit of a Rational Land Use Policy* (Master's thesis, Cornell University, 1977); Environmental Law Institute, *Conflict in the North Country* (Washington, D.C.: National Science Foundation, draft, 1979); or Holly Nelson and Alan J. Hahn, "State Policy and Local Influence in the Adirondacks" (Ithaca, N.Y.: Cornell University, Center for Environmental Research, September 1980). Recommendations of the Temporary State Commission to Study the Catskills are detailed in *The Future of the Catskills: Final Report* (Albany, N.Y.: April 1975). See also: Cynthia Dyballa, "Regionalism in the Catskills: A Political Analysis" (Ithaca, N.Y.: Cornell University Center for Environmental Research, June 1979); J. P. Kinney, "Backfire in the Catskills," *Empire State Report* (September 1975), p. 345.

37. Nelson and Hahn, "State Policy"; Dyballa, "Regionalism"; Alan J. Hahn and Cynthia D. Dyballa, "State Policy and Local Influence: A Comparison of Three Regional Natural Resource Management Agencies" (Ithaca, N.Y.: Cornell University Center for Environmental Research, 1980); and Cynthia Dyballa, "The Tug Hill Commission: A Cooperative Approach to Regional Planning" (Ithaca, N.Y.: Cornell University Center for Environmental Research, June 1979).

38. Watertown *Daily Times,* April 14, April 16, April 28, and May 6, 1970; and interview with Urban Karcher.

39. Watertown *Daily Times,* August 26, October 5, 1971. The six towns include: Highmarket, Lewis, Martinsburg, Montague, Osceola, and West Turin.

40. Watertown *Daily Times,* July 1, 1971.

41. Watertown *Daily Times,* September 23, October 5, 1971.

42. Watertown *Daily Times,* September 28, October 5, 1971; and interviews with Thomas Brown, Richard Mark, and John Wilson.

43. N.Y.S. Assembly Bill A.10541 (February 22, 1972); and N.Y.S. Senate Bill S.8877 (February 22, 1972).

44. New York State Office of Planning Services, "Memo: Assembly Bill No. 10541" (May 30, 1972).

45. New York State *Assembly Journal* (April 26, 1972); and New York State *Senate Journal* (May 4, 1972).

46. New York State, Laws of New York, Chapters 368 and 846 (1973) and Chapter 807 (1974).

Summary of Boundary Changes, Tug Hill Study Area

	Date	Jefferson	Lewis	Oneida	Oswego
Included in Original Legislation	1972	3 Towns	8 Towns	7 Towns	10 Towns
Added by Amendment	May 1973	Champion Adams Rutland Ellisburg Henderson	Denmark Leyden Lowville Turin	Boonville Floyd Steuben Trenton	Richland Sandy Creek
Removed by Amendment	June 1973	Watertown	Highmarket*		
	May 1973		Highmarket*		
	June 1973	Ellisburg Henderson			
	May 1974				Richland Sandy Creek
Current Towns	June 1974 on	7	12*	11	10

*The town of Highmarket, included in the original legislation, was consolidated into the town of West Turin in 1974, reducing the number of towns in the study area from forty to thirty-nine. With the pending merger, Highmarket was apparently prematurely removed in May 1973 and then added back in June.

47. H. E. Krueger, "The Lesser Wilderness: Tug Hill" (*N.Y.S. Conservationist,* February–March 1967), p. 22.

48. Interviews with Richard Mark and others.

49. Based on interviews with Champion officials.

50. New York State, Laws of New York, Chapter 972 (1972), p. 1.

51. Based on Commission's legislative history.

52. Temporary State Commission, *Newsletter* #1 (December 1973).

53. Watertown *Daily Times*, March 8, 1974.

54. SUNY, *Resources of the Tug Hill Region*.

55. Temporary State Commission, *Newsletter* #1 (December 1973).

56. Temporary State Commission, Minutes of Meeting (November 30, 1973).

57. Temporary State Commission, *Newsletter* #2 (February 1974).

58. Watertown *Daily Times*, February 28, 1974. This statement was made at the Lorraine forum, attended by 200 people.

59. Coe, *Citizen Participation*.

60. Temporary State Commission, *Interim Report* (March 1974).

61. Temporary State Commission, *Preliminary Findings*.

62. For public comments, see Exford, *Public Comments*. For revision of the recommendations, see Temporary State Commission, *Newsletter* #7 (November 1975), and *Preparing for the Future* (1976).

63. Temporary State Commission, *Preparing for the Future*.

64. Temporary State Commission, *Preparing for the Future*, p. 14.

3—THE TUG HILL COMMISSION: Its Program

1. Temporary State Commission on Tug Hill, "Request for Funding for Fiscal Year 1979–80" (Watertown, N.Y.: January 17, 1979).

2. Temporary State Commission on Tug Hill, *Preparing for the Future* (Watertown, N.Y.: February 1976), p. 14.

3. For a record of these public forums, see Benjamin Coe et al., *Citizen Participation in Tug Hill Studies* (Watertown, N.Y.: Temporary State Commission on Tug Hill, March 1975).

4. Temporary State Commission, *Preparing for the Future*, p. 34. For example, an early Tug Hill Commission memo, "A Possible Approach to Land Use Planning for Tug Hill" (1975), described a "tripartite local-region-state" land use policy, with: mandated local planning in an eighteen-month period; subregional groups to administer this planning; subregional administration of land use controls; and a regional body for approving developments of regional impact.

5. Benjamin Coe and Thornton Ware, "The Tug Hill Experience," *New York Planning Federation News* (March 1977), p. 4.

6. Northeast Regional Center for Rural Development, *The Proceedings of the Conference on Rural Land-Use Policy in the Northeast*, October 2–4, 1974, in Atlantic City, N.J. (Ithaca, N.Y.: February 1975).

7. Benjamin Coe et al., "Tug Hill Revisited," *New York Planning Federation News* (July–August 1979), p. 6.

8. Benjamin Coe, Testimony to New York State Assembly Ways and Means Committee (Watertown, N.Y.: Temporary State Commission on Tug Hill, September 27, 1979).

9. Benjamin Coe, "Tug Hill Revisited," p. 1.

10. The CTHPB's experience is described in Elizabeth Marsh, *Cooperative*

Rural Planning: A Tug Hill Case Study, draft (Pomona, N.J.: Stockton State College, 1979).

11. Cooperative Tug Hill Planning Board, *Model Rural Development Code* (Watertown, N.Y.: June 1977); and Cooperative Tug Hill Planning Board, *Tug Hill Resource Management Plan* (Watertown, N.Y.: September 1976).

12. Cooperative Tug Hill Planning Board, "Amendment to Intermunicipal Agreement" (March 8, 1979), and *Intermunicipal Agreement to Jointly Exercise Land Use Regulations* (December 1977). Quote from Benjamin Coe, "Tug Hill Revisited," p. 1.

13. Temporary State Commission on Tug Hill, *Newsletter* #5 (May 1975).

14. Since the pilot technical assistance program began, the Tug Hill Commission has recorded individual requests by subject matter, town or group filing the request, and date case was completed. Much information in this chapter is based on Commission technical assistance records from June 1975 to March 1980.

15. This program is described in the Commission's grant application, "Demonstration Program to Improve Management Skills and Upgrade Decision Making by Rural Local Officials, Phase II" (Watertown, N.Y.: May 5, 1978).

16. Benjamin Coe, "Evaluation of the Pilot Technical Assistance Program for Local Officials of Nine Rural Towns" (Watertown, N.Y.: Temporary State Commission on Tug Hill, July 19, 1978).

17. John Mason, "Public Service Employment Project Assistance, Spring of 1977" (Watertown, N.Y.: Temporary State Commission on Tug Hill, December 15, 1977). See Temporary State Commission, *Newsletter* #11 (November 1977), for a case history of the village of West Carthage's grant application for a picnic and boat launch area.

18. Temporary State Commission, *Newsletter* #9 (November 1976). Legislation referred to is New York State Freshwater Wetlands Act, Laws of New York, Chapter 614 (1975).

19. Temporary State Commission, *Newsletter* #14 (September 1979).

20. The National Science Foundation funded an eighteen-month project entitled "Preparing a Rural Public for Participation in Making Decisions about Science-based Issues" (December 1978–June 1980), for $29,830.

21. The U.S. Department of Health, Education, and Welfare funded a one-year project, "Communicating with a Rural Public on Environmental Issues in Decision Making" (July 1978–July 1980), for $25,000. The HEW project is evaluated in "Communicating with a Rural Public," a Tug Hill Commission report by Robert Quinn (September 15, 1979).

22. This and other statements in this section are based primarily on interviews with cooperative planning board members and Commission staff and on local newspaper accounts of the events described.

23. The seven water quality booklets are: *Water Cycle, Ground Water, Stream Quality, Types of Wetlands, Wetlands: Values to Man, Acid Rain,* and *Household Wastewater Management.* They were prepared by the State University Research Corporation at the State University of New York at Oswego (1979).

24. Elizabeth Marsh, *Cooperative Rural Planning.*

25. Success in this endeavor is described in Chapter 5. Not all towns and villages signed the IMA, despite this encouragement.

26. See, for example, Cooperative Tug Hill Planning Board, *Community Survey* (Watertown, N.Y.: May 1978); or Jefferson County Snowbelt Cooperative Planning Board, *Citizen Survey* (Watertown, N.Y.: April 1978).

27. This conference was aimed at those involved in local government, focusing on towns' and counties' roles in lake protection. Five co-sponsors included the Oneida Lake Association and the Herkimer-Oneida Water Quality Advisory Committee.

28. Temporary State Commission, Minutes of Meeting (Summer 1979).

29. Interviews with Richard Mark and others.

30. Temporary State Commission on Tug Hill, Minutes of Meeting (September 13, 1977).

31. The results of the November workshops are reported in Cornell University Cooperative Extension, *Results of Two Public Workshops on the Temporary State Commission on Tug Hill* (Ithaca, N.Y.: Cornell Cooperative Extension Community Resource Development Program, February 1980).

32. Information in this section about commissioners' backgrounds, opinions, and concerns is taken from interviews, Commission minutes, and information provided by Commission staff.

33. This was reported in interviews with area Cooperative Extension agents and local officials.

34. Temporary State Commission, Minutes of Meeting (May 9, 1973).

35. Chairman is used here and throughout this report, rather than chairperson, by request of the Commission. It should be noted that at least one woman chairs a cooperative planning board.

36. Information on staff backgrounds, structure, and arrangements with other agencies is based on interviews with staff in August 1979 and information provided by the Commission.

37. These two staff members were Donald Exford, who is still with the Commission, and Patrick Smyth.

38. The arrangement with Oneida County Planning Department, begun in 1979, provides service to the NEON planning board. The Commission pays 75 percent of the planner's salary. The arrangement with Black River-St. Lawrence Regional Planning and Development Board began in 1979. As of February 1980 the Oswego County Planning Department provides a planner to work with the NSCPB; the Commission pays 75 percent of his salary.

39. Budget data was provided by Benjamin Coe, Commission director. Some information in this section is based on interviews with state-level officials and staff.

40. The Cogar Foundation provided $6,000 in two grants; New York Cooperative Extension provided $3,000.

41. Based on budget information supplied by Benjamin Coe, Commission director.

42. Copies of these letters are in Tug Hill Commission files.

43. New York State Senate Bill S.1091-A (January 14, 1975). This bill was also introduced in the state assembly, but stayed in committee.

4—THE COMMISSION'S IMPACT: Cooperative Planning in Five Areas

1. Elizabeth Marsh has documented this process in her report, *Cooperative Rural Planning: A Tug Hill Case Study,* draft (Pomona, N.J.: Stockton State College, 1979).

2. Interview with Thornton Ware, Commission planning director (October 25, 1979).

3. The town of Lewis and the town/village of Turin requested admittance in 1979. The nine towns include: Boylston, Florence, Martinsburg, Montague, Osceola, Pinckney, Redfield, West Turin, and Worth.

4. The CTHPB area is described in: Cooperative Tug Hill Planning Board, *Tug Hill Resource Management Plan* (Watertown, N.Y.: September 1976); and State University College of Environmental Science and Forestry (SUNY), *Resources of the Tug Hill Region* (Syracuse, N.Y.: February 1974). Land ownership statistics for Redfield are based on 1979 property tax data assembled by the Commission.

5. Rome *Sentinel,* January 3, 1975.

6. Cooperative Tug Hill Planning Board, *Plan,* pp. 36–40.

7. Ibid., p. 3.

8. The Cogar Foundation provided two grants of $3,000 each; New York Cooperative Extension provided $3,000 for a community coordinator.

9. Frank Brown, "Cooperative Planning: A Venture of Nine Rural Towns," *New York Planning Federation News* (November–December 1977).

10. Cooperative Tug Hill Planning Board, *Plan,* p. 58. The plan lists implementation methods considered: public decision making and understanding, property tax reform, land easements and other similar arrangements, financial policy, and land use controls.

11. Cooperative Tug Hill Planning Board, *Model Rural Development Code* (Watertown, N.Y.: June 1977).

12. *Osceola Rural Development Code* (Watertown, N.Y.: 1977).

13. Cooperative Tug Hill Planning Board, *Intermunicipal Agreement to Jointly Exercise Land Use Regulations* (December 1977).

14. Donald Exford, "Report of Enforcement: 1978 Building Season" (Watertown, N.Y.: Cooperative Tug Hill Planning Board, 1979). Other information on enforcement supplied by the Tug Hill Commission staff and by interviews with participants.

15. Thornton Ware, "We don't Want Zoning Here!" *New York Planning Federation News* (July–August 1979), p. 5. Also, Cooperative Tug Hill Planning Board, *Intermunicipal Agreement.*

16. Thornton Ware, "We Don't Want Zoning Here!" pp. 4–5.

17. Salmon Rivers Cooperative Planning Board, *Comprehensive Regional Development Plan* (Watertown, N.Y.: 1979).

18. SRCPB towns and villages are described in: Salmon Rivers Cooperative Planning Board, *Plan*; and SUNY, *Resources of the Tug Hill Region.*

19. Based on interviews with SRCPB members and Commission staff and on Salmon Rivers Study Comparison Chart (1979) summarizing citizen surveys conducted.

20. Much of this section is based on minutes of SRCPB meetings and on interviews with SRCPB and town board members.

21. Temporary State Commission, *Newsletter* #9 (November 1976).

22. Salmon Rivers Survey Comparison Chart.

23. Salmon Rivers Cooperative Planning, *Plan.*

24. Interview with Eleanor Cusack, SRCPB chairman (August 11, 1979).

25. North Shore towns are described in: North Shore Cooperative Planning Board, *Existing Conditions* (Watertown, N.Y.: 1979); and SUNY, *Resources of the Tug Hill Region.* Oswego County growth projections were provided by Tug Hill Commission.

26. The work program was prepared by Pat Rountree, Commission planner for the NSCPB, and presented at the NSCPB's August 1979 meeting.

27. Based on interviews with Constantia residents and Commission staff; minutes of 1979 NSCPB and town planning board meetings; North Shore Cooperative Planning Board, *Existing Conditions,* pp. 27–30; and a chart prepared by Pat Rountree, Commission planner for NSCPB.

28. Information on JCSB towns was obtained from: interviews; information supplied by Commission staff; case studies of East Rodman, Adams Center, and Lorraine as part of Institute of Man and Science, *The Communities of the Tug Hill Region* (Rensselaerville, N.Y.: November 1974); JCSB, Minutes of Meetings (1977–79); and citizen surveys conducted by JCSB.

29. Jefferson County Snowbelt Cooperative Planning Board, Minutes of Meetings (1977–78).

30. Newspaper article by Rufus Chalmers, JCSB Chairman (1979), as part of the NSF/HEW citizen education project.

31. Temporary State Commission, *Newsletter* #8 (June 1976).

32. Assistance to Steuben was provided at its request, in an effort to bring the town's planning and land use regulation capabilities to the same level as the other three towns. See, for example, Steuben Town Planning Board, *Comprehensive Plan* (1978), and Citizen Survey Results (January 1977).

33. SEQR meeting, October 1979. A November 1979 meeting for town clerks, zoning board of appeals members, and enforcement officers to discuss mutual enforcement problems was cancelled for lack of interest.

34. Based on interviews, and on attendance at the November 1979 workshops, described in Cornell University Cooperative Extension, *Results of Two Public Workshops on the Temporary State Commission on Tug Hill* (Ithaca, N.Y.: Cornell Cooperative Extension Community Resource Development Program, February 1980).

5—THE COMMISSION'S IMPACT: How Significant Are Its Accomplishments

1. Benjamin Coe et al., "Tug Hill Revisited," *New York Planning Federation News* (1979), p. 1.

2. This review, it should be noted, was conducted before the Temporary Commission's projected phase-out of March 31, 1981.

3. The information in this chapter is largely based on interviews conducted with nearly sixty cooperative planning board members, local officials, commissioners and staff, and other interested parties. Quotes are not attributed to individuals by name to protect the confidentiality of interviews.

4. No cooperative planning board members were interviewed in the NEON area.

5. Cornell University Cooperative Extension, *Results of Two Public Workshops on the Temporary State Commission on Tug Hill* (Ithaca, N.Y.: Cornell University Cooperative Extension Community Resource Development Program, February 1980). Other references to the November 1979 workshops in this section are based on this report and on author's notes taken during attendance at the two workshops.

6. This view, described in the Commission's 1976 report, *Preparing for the Future*, was confirmed by interviews and by other documents.

7. The original interviews with these legislators were conducted in the fall and winter of 1979.

8. Cooperative Tug Hill Planning Board, *Model Rural Development Code* (Watertown, N.Y.: 1977).

9. E. Baumann, *Analysis of Land Use Planning on Tug Hill* (Watertown, N.Y.: Temporary State Commission on Tug Hill, 1974); and Benjamin Coe et al., *Land Use Policy Development in the Rural Tug Hill Area of New York State* (Watertown, N.Y.: Temporary State Commission on Tug Hill, September 1976), 3:36–38.

10. Information supplied by Commission staff. Legislation referred to is New York State Freshwater Wetlands Act, Laws of New York, Chapter 614, 1975.

11. Montague Town Board, *Interim Zoning Ordinance* (July 1976).

12. Donald Exford, "Report of Enforcement: 1978 Building Season" (Watertown, N.Y.: Cooperative Tug Hill Planning Board, 1979).

13. Institute of Man and Science, *The Communities of the Tug Hill Region* (Rensselaerville, N.Y.: 1974), pp. 11–12.

14. Based on interviews with Benjamin Coe and CTHPB officials.

15. Cooperative Tug Hill Planning Board, *Community Survey* (Watertown, N.Y.: November 1976).

16. Lewis County Legislature, *Resolution #34* (1978).

17. Bert Swift, *Planning for Local Development: The Case of Oneida-Herkimer Counties* (Ithaca, N.Y.: New York State Cooperative Extension, March 1972).

18. Temporary State Commission on Tug Hill, with Jefferson County Planning Board and Black River-St. Lawrence Regional Planning and Development Board, "Joint Statement: Beliefs Concerning the Process of Preparing for the Future" (Watertown, N.Y.: September 13, 1978). Also *Intercom* (Newsletter of Black River-St. Lawrence Regional Planning Board) 5, no. 5 (1978), p. 3.

19. Temporary State Commission on Tug Hill, *Preparing for the Future* (Watertown, N.Y.: February 1976), p. 12.

20. Cornell University Cooperative Extension, *Two Public Workshops* (February 1980).

6—LESSONS FOR OTHER RURAL AREAS

1. American Law Institute, as quoted in Michael Kintner, *In Pursuit of A Rational Land Use Policy* (Master's thesis, Cornell University, 1977), p. 289.

2. Council of State Planning Agencies, *State Development Strategies for Rural Communities,* State Planning Series, no. 6 (1977), pp. 14, 29.

3. *The Carter Administration, Small Community and Rural Development Policy* (The White House: December 20, 1979), p. 37.

4. Robert G. Healy, *Land Use and the States* (Washington, D.C.: Resources for the Future, 1976), p. 6.

5. Interview with Elizabeth Marsh, professor at Stockton State College, Pomona, N.J., October 1979.

Index

THE TUG HILL PROGRAM

was composed in 10-point Mergenthaler Times Roman on a Linotron 202,
and leaded two points by Eastern Graphics;
printed on 55-pound Glatfelter Offset Vellum,
adhesive bound, with covers printed by Frank A. West Company, Inc. on Corvon 220-13,
by Maple-Vail Book Manufacturing Group, Inc.;
and published by

SYRACUSE UNIVERSITY PRESS

SYRACUSE NEW YORK, 13210